SPIRITED LI

SPIRITED LIVING
Waging Conflict, Building Peace

Simon Fisher

SWARTHMORE LECTURE 2004
QUAKER BOOKS

First published in May 2004 by Quaker Books
Friends House, Euston Road, London NW1 2BJ

http://www.quaker.org.uk

© Simon Fisher

ISBN 0 85245 357 4

Design & typesetting: Jonathan Sargent
Printed and bound by Halstan & Co Ltd, Amersham
Text typeface: Kuenstler 480, 10.5 pt
Cover design: Golden Cockerel Press Ltd
Cover illustration: *Forming Spirits* by Carol Baker
Extract from *The Cure at Troy* by permission of Faber and
Faber Ltd

DEDICATION

This book is dedicated to Jane, my wife, who is my deepest love, my strongest rock, and most demanding critic.

History says, Don't hope
On this side of the grave.
But then, once in a life time
The longed-for tidal wave
Of justice can rise up,
And hope and history rhyme.

So hope for a great sea change
On the far side of revenge.
Believe that a further shore
Is reachable from here.
Believe in miracles
And cures and healing wells

. . .

If there's fire on the mountain
Or lightning and storm
And a god speaks from the sky

That means someone is hearing
The outcry and the birth-cry
Of new life at its term.

Seamus Heaney
from *The Cure at Troy* 1990

About the Author

Simon Fisher is a founder and co-director of Responding to Conflict (RTC), a Birmingham-based charity working internationally for peace and justice. RTC works with people striving for social and political change in their own societies. In the past, Simon has been responsible for building RTC's international training and support programme, with a particular emphasis on Afghanistan, the Balkans, Israel/Palestine and East/Central Africa. He is now engaged primarily in developing ACTS (Applied Conflict Transformation Studies), a practical global programme being developed initially with regional learning centres in Phnom Penh, Belgrade, Accra and Kampala. His earlier background was in education and development and he was Oxfam Country Representative in Zaire (now the Democratic Republic of Congo) from 1986–90.

A Quaker since 1976, Simon and his wife Jane were Quaker Peace & Service representatives in Southern Africa. Simon has co-authored several books in the fields of education and conflict transformation, and is Honorary Research Fellow at Bradford University Department of Peace Studies.

As co-author

Debate and Decision: schools in a world of change, Robin Richardson, Marion Flood, Simon Fisher, One World Trust, 1980

Ideas into Action: curriculum for a changing world, Simon Fisher, Frances Magee, James Wetz, One World Trust, 1981

World Studies 8–13: a teacher's handbook, Simon Fisher and David Hicks, Oliver and Boyd, 1986

Working with Conflict: skills and strategies for action, Simon Fisher, Dekha Ibrahim Abdi, Jawed Ludin, Richard Smith, Steve Williams, Sue Williams, Zed Publications/ Responding to Conflict, 2000 (reprinted 2003, and translated into French, Spanish, Russian, Georgian, Bahasa Indonesia)

As co-editor

Transforming Conflict: reflections of practitioners worldwide, Action for Conflict Transformation, 2003.

CONTENTS

Diagrams

CONTENTS

PREFACE

The Swarthmore Lectureship was established by the Woodbrooke Extension Committee at a meeting held December 9, 1907: the minute of the Committee providing for an 'annual lecture on some subject relating to the message and work of the Society of Friends'. The name Swarthmore was chosen in memory of the home of Margaret Fox, which was always open to the earnest seeker after Truth, and from which loving words of sympathy and substantial material help were sent to fellow workers.

The lectureship has a twofold purpose: first, to interpret to the members of the Society of Friends their message and mission; and secondly, to bring before the public the spirit, the aims and fundamental principles of Friends. The lecturers alone are responsible for any opinions expressed.

The lectureship provides both for the publication of a book and for the delivery of a lecture, the latter usually at the time of assembly of Britain Yearly Meeting of the Society of Friends. A lecture related to the present book was delivered at Yearly Meeting in London on the evening of May 29, 2004.

The Swarthmore Lecture Committee can be contacted via the Clerk, c/o Woodbrooke Quaker Study Centre, 1046 Bristol Road, Selly Oak, Birmingham B29 6LJ.

For assistance in the preparation of this book, the Swarthmore Lecture Committee wishes to thank The William P. Bancroft and Jenepher Gillet Trust, The George Cadbury 'A' Fund, and The W. F. Southall Trust.

FOREWORD

You will say, Christ saith this, and the apostles say this;
but what canst thou say? Art thou a child of the Light
and hast walked in the Light, and what thou speakest is
it inwardly from God?

George Fox, quoted by Margaret Fell
(Quaker faith & practice §19.07)

This book is written by an activist taking time out. It is not primarily
for academics, or experts in the field. It is more for all those of us
who are concerned, and sometimes alarmed, by the alienation and
violence we see around us and the way it impinges increasingly on our
lives. It seeks to offer signposts to a greater sense of clarity about how
we can be agents of change, true to the spirit of love and compassion,
and – for Quakers – to the origins of the Society of Friends. It suggests that peace work today requires us to become signs of
contradiction, rebels in our own society, and seeks to deepen our
awareness of what this could mean in practical terms. Questions are
raised throughout the book about our own stance and how this measures up to the prevalent culture of violence in which we live.

What canst thou say?

The task of writing the book has led me to wonder, profoundly, what
I have discovered at first hand about conflict and peace. 'What canst
thou say?' has been an incessant internal question. To separate out the
proffered wisdoms and axioms of others, known and unknown, that
one has accepted for better or worse in the haste of life, to test each in
the heat of one's own experience, and then to have these tested again
by the members of the committee and others, Quakers and non-
Quakers, who have offered to accompany me on this journey, this
has been gruelling.

It has also been, ultimately, profoundly enlightening, and encouraging. There were moments of anxiety, early on, when the worm-like

thought insinuated itself: maybe I have nothing authentic to say, or, more worryingly, maybe I am artfully reframing, for a moral audience, a life experience dedicated to pleasure. For I have had, and continue to have enormous enjoyment in this work and the friends I have the good fortune to work with and to visit, even in the midst of dislocation and insecurity. How much laughter we have, how much pleasure in each other's company. Let no one say that peace work is only serious and solemn. It is, in my experience, also inseparable from 'the bright side of life' as the Monty Python song goes.

How canst thou say it?

More recently in the progress of this book, I have faced the problem of communication. How to speak truth, as I experience it, to members of the British Quaker community, and to others beyond, so that it can be understood. It is as though, for the last few years, my work has taken me out of the zone of normality in which most people live. Visits to valiant colleagues in Afghanistan, Zimbabwe, Uganda, Israel and Palestine in the time leading up to this book have been full of urgency, passion, endurance, hope and grief. Despair is always silently at the door, never acknowledged. My sense of inadequacy in the face of this is sometimes agonising, and ultimately isolating.

I have, I suppose, been living almost constantly beyond the social comfort zone for a long time. As a result, I find it hard to connect with neighbours and friends in the times when I am at home, and they with me. The conversation often begins with a question: 'Where have you been then?' Followed rapidly by: 'Where are you going next?' The journeys themselves have some common currency. People travel: they know what long flights and bus journeys entail. But what happens on these journeys, what they are about, is a mystery to nearly all. With very few exceptions, people outside the precious circles of family and work colleagues no longer ask. And if they do, it is almost impossible to explain in a way which conveys something real.

How to describe a visit to Afghanistan in the midst of planning this book? Friends with whom I have been working for over ten years have mutated in a few brief months from community development workers to ministers and top officials. Kabul, the capital, is utterly desolate, and the government, with desperately few means, struggles to meet even the most basic needs of the people there and in the rural areas. My friends are upbeat, pleased at last to be struggling for something they see as valuable, rather than to be coping with the Taliban regime. They are pleased too that the US chose to invade Afghanistan, and we have a difficult discussion over US global strategic aims. Such contacts compel a challenge to western liberal consensus.

Or how to describe a meeting shortly beforehand in Kampala with chiefs, religious leaders and community workers from a war zone in northern Uganda? They had travelled over 400 kilometres to Kampala, over bandit-ridden roads, as I did not, this time, have the chance to go to see them. They were updating me on what had happened since my last working visit to them. Although the war had intensified, and the rebels had the previous day blown up a public bus with a landmine, these friends, and their organisations, have been very active in peacebuilding. They have, for example, been actively lobbying the government to engage in peace talks and running peace education programmes in their schools and the surrounding villages. At this particular moment they are engaged in a major mediation initiative. They are now determined to start a peace institute in their town, a project they feel will mobilise people in a way not so far possible.

Although those who can have now sent their children out of town because of the imminent dangers, they remain full of hope, and commitment. We discuss some possibilities, and make some plans.

I am left with the inadequacy of my response, at a human as well as professional level, in the face of such indomitable heroism in Kampala and Kabul. How does one with equanimity leave such situations, pack one's bags and head for the airport? How does one speak of it at home and be understood? How does that reality touch, and inform, that of my home town, Birmingham?

Writing this book is in part an attempt to explain and depict different realities with which I have come into contact in a way which allows them, and the underlying context, to be understood, to disturb and empower. Where I have skated too fast over a complex idea or argument, please forgive me, and look in the recommended reading for more. My hope is that my realities will connect and combine with

those experienced by members of the Society and other readers, and
that the mix will prove – nonviolently – explosive.

ACKNOWLEDGEMENTS

First I owe a debt to a country, Algeria, where I was a VSO volunteer and from which I was twice forcibly expelled by the time I was twenty. The first occasion, in 1967, was a result of the UK's alleged involvement on the Israeli side in the Yom Kippur war. The second, a year later, was under prosecution for indecent exposure, after I had effected an innocent, if rapid, change into bathing trunks behind the all-too-transparent screen of a car door. My political, cultural and religious awareness was changed for ever.

I am deeply grateful to the people who have helped me write this lecture. The Swarthmore Committee, in the form of Pam Lunn and Ruth Heine, have guided and supported me. My splendid colleagues at Responding to Conflict in Birmingham are a continual source of joy and strength. All of them have helped, especially Mary Lou Leavitt and Bridget Walker, whose ideas have challenged and informed me deeply. The global RTC family is a constant source of inspiration, mingled with anguish. Jennifer Barraclough and Val Ferguson critiqued and encouraged, Howard and Esther Boyd, Roswitha Jarman and Emma Leslie gave advice and ideas, staff at Friends House went out of their way to be helpful, as did Mary Ellen McNish, of American Friends Service Committee.

Further back, Adam Curle's 1971 Swarthmore Lecture set me alight and Nicholas Gillett provided crucial opportunities for the fire to burn freely. There have been many other dear companions on the way, including: Sidney and Brenda Bailey, Neil Jameson, Richard and Pushpa Knottenbelt, Graham Davey, Robin Richardson, Dave Hicks, Gratien and Marie Bivegete, Dudu Mtshazo, H.W. van der Merwe, Prosper Bulemvu, Vesna Matovic, Michael Appleby, Bunty Biggs, Rosalba Oywa, Sheelagh Willett, Chris Barber, Diana Francis, Judith Large, Steve and Sue Williams, Dekha Ibrahim Abdi, Joy Cheek. Jane, my wife, and our offspring, Naomi, Jonah, Abigail and Susannah, have taught me more than I know, and tested my certainties with affectionate insistence.

The shortcomings in this book are, of course, all mine.

SPIRITED LIVING

INTRODUCTION

A seed which flourished

Wind fills the sails. The yacht careens in sunshine towards the horizon, apparently oblivious to a massive bank of dark clouds, towards which it is speeding.

This little picture, a postcard, sent to me long ago by a friend, sits on the windowsill of my office. On the facing wall, another picture, hand drawn by colleagues. This time of a much smaller boat, filled with several anxiously rowing people, heading remorselessly, and with a severe list, for a waterfall. Will they avoid it? The caption reads: 'Is it always like this at Responding to Conflict?'

The first picture I often look at – a source of comfort: look how the boat is angled to catch the full weight of the wind, how confidently it sails out to meet the storm. The second I rarely look at, though visitors tend to see it rather quickly. It has no colour, it is not especially pleasing to the eye, and, well, the message is not a very positive one, perhaps, if one is supposed to have a hand on the tiller, which, as a co-director of Responding to Conflict (RTC), I am.

But it is this second picture which makes me think the most: about where we are going, certainly, but also about how we got here.

On that first day of RTC's existence, in September 1991, I found myself alone in a small, empty room at Woodbrooke, in the company of an untested idea and enough money for a few months. Was it all a ghastly mistake? In the past, I had been in at the start of a number of peace-related initiatives, but this was maybe one step too far. Certainly it had not been easy to persuade funders to back the idea. And with four growing children to look after, my wife Jane and I needed to earn enough to keep them fed and clothed. We had been living in Africa for most of the previous ten years, and were now in a city where we knew few people.

Today, RTC has long burst out of that room. With a (deliberately) small staff and an unnumbered, farflung constituency of friends and colleagues, RTC is supporting cross-cultural peacebuilding and conflict transformation initiatives in many parts of the world. Its international courses are well-subscribed, its handbook and video case studies have travelled widely into different regions and languages. Vigorous, now independent, networks of activists have grown up in the company of RTC in Afghanistan, Africa, East Asia and at global level. Continuing programmes of practical support and accompaniment are underway, primarily in Israel-Palestine, Central/South Asia and East/Central Africa. A collaborative, and combative, spirit links RTC staff and associates with former course participants and friends, who work together to address common issues, whether at individual or global level.

The seed which emerged uncertainly in that empty room has flowered and propagated in quite unexpected ways. There was no strategic plan which foresaw all this. There is no single person who can claim ownership or credit: it has happened through the coming together of many activists and supporters. And because of this, because the plant grew as it needed to, untidily, unpredictably and at varying speeds, progress has never been certain, the future has always seemed unsure, and the pressure on staff and trustees, whose lives have been most closely caught up with RTC, has sometimes been exhausting, almost unbearable.

Some, at least, of the soil was initially cultivated in Zaire (now Democratic Republic of Congo). During four years there as Country Representative for Oxfam I found myself often facing the corrupt and repressive powers of Mobutu's state apparatus. From the ridiculous (his ministers used Oxfam's import licence to buy in fifty cases of champagne) to the annoying (impounding an order for four campbeds deemed to be 'military supplies') to the dangerous (interrogation at gunpoint) there was never any lack of interest. But neither was there any advice to speak of, to deal with these situations or the plenteous conflicts within Oxfam, rooted in profound differences of perspective amongst the staff.

On my return to the UK I found that other staff were faced with the same difficulty. Dealing with conflict and violence was not considered part of Oxfam's mandate. During a three month consultancy that followed, it emerged that Oxfam's situation was typical of other international agencies. Peace work was off-limits for most relief and development agencies – unless it was a matter of liberation struggles, which had often received support during the 1970s and 1980s. And yet conflict and instability were becoming more prevalent in the world as the old Cold War order changed.

The urge to do something to remedy this took hold when I settled back in the UK. With a substantial family there was a need to earn money and stay in one place for a bit. I applied for a number of jobs which I was well qualified for, and found myself unable to follow through. I under-performed at interview, under pressure from my internal mentor. If I felt I was near to being chosen I withdrew before the verdict could be announced.

What to do? No single individual or organisation could know the answers to the problems of building peaceful and just societies, that was clear. Differing culture, context and values ensure that each of us has to work these out for ourselves anew, building on the raw material available. So there was no package of solutions to be found and then dispensed. But if, the hypothesis ran, seasoned activists could come together who were working for peace and justice in their own societies, they could effectively teach each other. RTC could provide a safe space and a careful process for this to happen in a coherent, cumulative fashion and assist with synthesising ideas and plans for follow-up action. Hopefully they would leave having found new and creative ways to address their problems. So the plan evolved to offer a long (eleven weeks) course in which all this could happen organically.

When two Quaker trusts bravely made some initial resources available, Jane and I moved house, with our four children, from Bristol to Birmingham: Woodbrooke had offered to provide an office for a low rent, and the Selly Oak Colleges Federation was an obvious home, with its range of practical international courses.

Initially it seemed we might not be successful. We produced a leaflet and sent it to all our friends, to the friends of friends, to every organisation listed in *Housmans Peace Diary*. There was plenty of advice that the idea was unrealistic. This was not the right time for such an initiative.

There was a long silence. Then, as it began to seem that the doubters might be right, people began to respond, from all over the world: human rights and development workers, priests, journalists, imams, educators, doctors, people with no label but a record of real engagement. And when it became clear that enough people had applied, with enough sponsorship, for the first course to take place, another hurdle presented itself. How could a course be designed to cater for such a variety of people and expectations? There was nothing quite like it anywhere. Again, a feeling of inadequacy swept in, but it was matched at the same time by a power that would brook no escape, a commitment which seemed to come from beyond to find a solution. And, crucially, people began to emerge with the necessary experience and skills to make the course run.

They have done so ever since, paid and unpaid, from all the continents and many countries. Many former course participants have gone on to empower and teach others: for example, the current tutors of the Working with Conflict course are all from their ranks.

Where does the passion come from?

What follows in this book arises out of the experience of RTC, and other, earlier occasions when my sails have somehow caught the wind. It also comes deeply from my Quaker origins and leanings. Brought up an Anglican in a family with a strong military tradition, I was accustomed, as a child, to playing the organ in the regimental church. Our family stood solemnly each year for the Queen's Christmas speech. I was in my twenties when branded a Pelagian heretic by a priest in the Anglican Church of Rhodesia and the latent fires of nonconformity were stoked. Shortly afterwards I discovered that I had Quaker antecedents, in the form of a 100 year old great aunt, who turned out to be related to William Allen, the nineteenth-century Friend known as a physicist and philanthropist. Having already found Friends independently by then, this came as a powerful affirmation of my roots.

The experience I am trying to convey is not easily amenable to words: it is of being inspired, inhabited by a passionate, intuitive vision. It is a potentially dangerous condition which, in its impetuosity and overwhelming yearning, has the seeds of its own destruction.

Yet, in its raw energy is found some of the essential fuel for far-reaching, spirit-led change. Fortunately, in my limited experience at least, when the moment is ripe, others come to provide other essentials: the holding, the companionship, the challenge and the enlightening, restraining wisdom.

Where does the passion come from? It is hard to articulate what comes from another, literally unspeakable, place deep within, but I have tried below to express something of how I see it.

We are essentially creatures of balance, of harmony. My body is composed of billions of cells, growing, replacing themselves. My life is sustained by myriad people providing for my needs, and I for theirs. The planet provides, unasked and usually unacknowledged, the air, the ground, the space to live and love. The endeavours of many people in the past, especially my parents, and their parents, have made my life possible, and as enjoyable as it is. 'I' am a miraculous conjunction of all these things, in this moment of time and space.

The table on which I am writing, it too is a momentary creature, a universe in itself. Without seed, sun, rain, and soil no tree would have grown. Who cut the tree, transported it, shaped it? Who found and mined the iron-ore for the screws? Who manufactured them? If we take these component parts away, there is no table.

I am one with the table, with the universe. We exist as a complex of many parts, for a moment, in which life and death are inextricable companions.

'A person who looks at a table and can see the universe is a person who can see the way' says Thich Nhat Hanh in *The Miracle of Mindfulness* (Hanh, 1987).

Most of us see reality in little sections. Once we see it as a whole, we realise that the person we think of as our 'self' is not a fixed entity, but fluid and intangible. To build up our public selves, to defend our little selves against reality out there, is pointless. Our essence, our purpose, is to be in balance and harmony with the world out there, and within our selves. The 'promptings of love and truth' come from the deepest wells of life, from God, if you will. They constitute our guide. Living like this we are liberated from fear, hatred, suffering. Living like this is fulfilment itself. Living like this we are, finally, healthy.

But today, most days, I am ill at ease. Dis-eased. I have no fever or headache. No doctor would diagnose me as sick. Yet my experience is of imbalance, distress. It comes, as many others have realised before me, from the fact that while I am in essence a creature of balance and harmony, I am living in a world where imbalance and suffering are everywhere. I cannot cut myself off from this without constructing artificial barriers, for example by ignoring events in the wider world. Many try, but in my case I know this would prevent me from being healthy and fulfilled. And even in artificial ignorance I would be out of balance.

So I search for equilibrium, for a reduction of suffering, out of my own, profound, inner need. I do this for myself as much as for others. I feel it sometimes as agony, and weep, for no apparent reason. More usually it manifests as compassion, and sometimes simply as passion. (Both words have their origin in the Latin word *pati* = to suffer.)

To cure myself, to find health, I must work to alleviate those sources of dis-ease and misery in the world outside. In the doing of it, however successfully or not, and in joining with myriad others in this struggle, laughter joins with the tears, creativity and hope dance once more. We become whole again.

Peace work is for me essentially this. It is about joining with others to restore the wholeness, balance and harmony which are at the base of our existence. It is work for all times, for all levels: personal, inter-personal, community, nation and globe. While I can work at any level, I will try to combine the individual and the wider levels: the personal and the political. Without the personal I will be forgetting the only individual I am ultimately responsible for. Without the political I risk indulging my false self, and missing the challenge to influence the way things are done, and to whom.

One thing I know. This harmony, this balance, is a delicate thing. It is as sensitive and vulnerable as a single human being. I cannot eliminate an injustice by resisting, or imposing, with violence or force of arms, without creating further damage. Nor, equally, by accepting silently whatever is done to me, or to others in my name. Both paths bring more distress and destruction, sooner or later. Peace work is the art of finding ways to live in the present in a manner which will create a more just and equitable future. Peace work learns from experience but has no blueprints. It thrives on creativity, determination, love, and fun. It is a continual adventure.

But what of the present? What do these experiences, and the resulting insights, say about our witness and response as Friends to a world marked indelibly by the violent conflict in Iraq in 2003? We are citizens of a country where invasion has been renamed war, occupation is re-clothed as liberation, and unilateral action deemed essential to defend the honour of a decidedly unconvinced – and unavoidably multilateral – United Nations. We have worn 'Not in my Name' badges, written and signed countless letters and petitions, held vigils and marched in vast numbers, taken part in die-ins and direct action. How do we face our apparent powerlessness? What do we learn about effective peace witness from all of this?

As I stare, now, at the pictures of the two boats on my office wall, speeding headlong, I am filled with a mixture of hope and apprehension. We are moving into a world where to speak and act for peace and justice will be increasingly controversial. We will be ridiculed, ignored, denigrated as unpatriotic. The rhetoric of threat and the creation of invisible enemies to replace the 'red peril' have built up steadily, to the point that many feel afraid. And when we are afraid, when our security feels weak, we can justify most things, including the mistreatment of asylum seekers and the indefinite holding of children as prisoners in Guantanamo Bay. And, in the face of all this, how hard it is to resist, to stand out, isolated, from our tribe.

Yet the challenge is clearer than it has been for a long time. We cannot know, any of us, where precisely we are going, but we can be sure that the uncertain and risky course we set, in faith, offers undreamed of possibilities. For each of us, to live adventurously will mean something different. But to head for the shore, to prioritise safety, career, a pension perhaps, never has been an option, morally or practically, for Quakers, or peacemakers in any generation. We are heirs to an irresistible tradition, out of which this lecture springs.

1

Questions arising

A loss of clarity and confidence

Richard knew where he stood. He took part in public demonstrations for justice and peace. He would not join the armed forces. He refused even to fill in tax forms where he had to describe himself as belonging to one race or another. As a result he was imprisoned for a period. His access to jobs was restricted. He was ostracised by members of the white community, all the more for marrying Pushpa, a woman of Indian descent. This in turn led to Pushpa's separation from her family.

He was one of the first freedom fighters I ever met. He was also a Quaker. Under Ian Smith's regime in the 1970s Zimbabwe – then Southern Rhodesia – was an illegal and racist state and the issues were clear. The challenge for a Quaker well versed in the peace testimony, and in the history of Quakers' witness for peace, was equally clear. Acquiesce in the status quo, hoping things would change in due course, or take a stand and bear the cost?

Today's Zimbabwe is equally militarised and oppressive, with similarly questionable legality. The small governing group is forcing its will on the majority. Richard is still in Zimbabwe, with his wife Pushpa, still teaching maths in a secondary school, as he was thirty years ago. But his response has to take account of more contradictions: he is not being called up to fight, just expected to acquiesce as his friends and the population as a whole suffer deprivation and harrassment. He is a white Zimbabwean, still with a lifestyle most black citizens would envy, modest though it is. If he stands out against what is happening there will be consequences. How does he express his stand for truth, peace and justice now? Where are the certainties?

Richard's dilemma mirrors that faced now by the wider Religious Society of Friends, and by many others with similar values. Quakers are known widely for our active commitment to peace. The Peace

Testimony – a touchstone of what it means to be a Quaker for members and outsiders alike – has led Friends from the earliest times to be peacemakers: sometimes making a stand on principle themselves, sometimes bringing relief to those suffering from violence and war, sometimes actively engaging in peace creation. Quakers brought relief supplies and friendship to devastated people in post-war Germany in 1945. They were conscientious objectors in both world wars and more recently, in the Peace Tax campaign, contested the right of government to make citizens pay taxes for defence against their will. It has led them to involvement in many campaigns, including those against the arms trade, nuclear weapons and child soldiers. It has led to Quaker involvement in international mediation at international level, for example in Nigeria, Pakistan, the Middle East and Zimbabwe.

But now, perhaps especially since the early 1990s, it seems as though we have lost the assurance we had earlier. The issues seem more complex. Preventive measures – such as saying 'No' to taxes or military service, and third party intervention to stop violent conflict between other countries – highly worthwhile though they all were and remain, seem not to have more than temporary effect, or, more crucially, to lack the depth to constitute an adequate response to the growing incidence of injustice and violent conflict, both in the wider world and in Britain's own cities and neighbourhoods. Aid for the casualties of war and other calamities is now provided by many relief and development agencies (some of them founded by Quakers of an earlier generation). Active peace work is now undertaken by the same agencies, and by others started specifically to develop in practical form this new field of conflict transformation.

This lack of clarity about an appropriate peace witness has not dimmed Quakers' deep commitment to it as a fundamental aspect of the Society's witness to truth, but it has seemingly led to a loss of cohesiveness, a bewilderment about where to stand. Is there any more a distinctive role for us on peace? Quakers, as represented in Britain Yearly Meeting, have arguably allowed our peace-related programmes to diminish in both scope and impact, just as the incidence and nature of violent conflict in the world has been changing, and coming closer to home.

Certainly there are still vigorous signs of life at the level of individuals, who are engaged in a huge variety of related issues. There are innovative new programmes – as evidenced by Turning the Tide's work on active nonviolence, for example, which provides training for a wide range of activists addressing nuclear weapons and other issues in Britain and overseas. There is also the LEAP initiative, which works with young, often disadvantaged people on many aspects of life, including conflict resolution.

But there is a wider, and deeper, loss of confidence and direction. Internationally the number of workers sponsored by Friends has reduced substantially, for good or ill, and work from London in support of international mediation has decreased, though similar bridge-building work is still strongly supported by the Quaker United Nations offices in Geneva and New York.

Internally, within Britain, members of the Society wanting to work in their own neighbourhoods talk of being paralysed by guilt. How can they, largely white, relate effectively to black and Asian communities? Should they be doing more to build bridges with Muslims? Are Quakers inevitably on the 'wrong side', at the same time feeling alienated in belief and attitude from much of the majority community?

In my experience, many younger Friends now interpret their commitment to peace in largely personal terms. It has a major influence on how they deal with other people, what jobs they feel they should, or should not, take, how they deal with everyday conflicts, but for many, the political dimension, our role as citizens in a country with internal tensions and an international role and wars on the agenda, is not there. This alienation from the big picture appears to be true also of young people more generally in Britain. They mostly do not vote and do not join political parties. The proportion of students taking university courses in environmental and ecological studies is declining, although the state of the environment cries out for engagement.

The bedrock: testimonies to peace and equality

Thus Quakers are in some confusion. Born into an undoubtedly great tradition and a historic experience of struggle from the earliest times, we are searching for a new vision. In the mid-seventeenth century,

when the Society was born, everything was in flux. The House of
Commons had rebelled against Charles I, the monarchy had been
abolished and the monarch executed. The House of Lords had been
abolished. In 1661 one third of the total male membership of the
Society (4,257) were in prison on suspicion of being part of the Fifth
Monarchy uprising. It was out of this turmoil that the first document
emerged from Friends concerning peace – though the reason was in
fact to deny charges of disloyalty to Charles II rather than make a
statement about peace witness as we now understand it. It was at
this moment that Fox wrote, in a long document: 'We do utterly deny
…all outward wars and strife and fightings with outward weapons,
for any end or under any pretence whatsoever.'

It is this conviction which has developed into what we call our peace
testimony today. It says clearly to us, and all who seek to join us or
know more, that we refuse to fight wars. We will not use weapons of
war, or willingly allow them to be used in our name. We are called to
resolve conflicts, at whatever level, without violence. We are prepared
to pay the ultimate cost – our lives if necessary – to uphold this conviction, which comes from our deepest roots, that everyone has within
them something of God which is sacred. We can never deliberately
destroy a person without at the same time destroying a part of God.

It is this conviction that every person has 'that of God' within
them which has given rise to our equally powerful testimony to equality. From the earliest times Quakers were persecuted for refusing to
doff their hats, or use titles to address others deemed more worthy of
respect.

At the same time Quakers saw that others, less advantaged, should
have the benefits and freedoms they themselves were able to enjoy.
They after all have the same share of God's truth, the same 'spark'.
This conviction has fuelled an enduring commitment to fight poverty
and to take part in the struggle for equal rights for people who are
oppressed.

If the peace testimony, then, informs us of *how* we need to conduct
ourselves in conflicts, whether our own or as third parties in the conflicts of others, our testimony to equality shows us a crucial area
where we need to apply it. Not only where there is open warfare, but

also where there is deprivation and suffering, which are very often the result of hidden or suppressed conflict.

Apartheid South Africa was an instance of suppressed conflict in which Quakers became actively engaged, out of these dual convictions: the need for justice and to avoid a bloody war. I still remember the surreal feeling I had in 1983 when, as newly appointed Quaker Peace and Service Representative with my wife Jane, visiting top civil servants in Cape Town in the company of H.W. van der Merwe, a prominent Afrikaner Quaker who was trying to help us obtain a visa to live and work in South Africa. As we sat in deep leather armchairs and drank tea from delicate bone china cups H.W., who had been to school with many of the nationalist pillars of apartheid and was still friends with them, pleaded our cause with an urbane man who would not have been out of place in the most exclusive of London clubs, or in Downing Street. Finally, after listening exhaustively to H.W.'s entreaties, often in Afrikaans, the man turned to me and said, in a perfectly friendly manner: 'Let me check. I think you are asking me to allow you to come into this country in order to overthrow our system. What sort of a Religious Society *are* you?' The small, perhaps 300 strong, group of Quakers in Southern Africa made a disproportionate impact on the political changes that took place, often at considerable cost to themselves, and they remain deeply engaged.

Through the centuries, the level of engagement by members of the Society has risen and fallen. If our past, joined with that of the many others who have witnessed bravely to peace and justice, offers much to inspire us, what, we may ask, do we have now to guide us as we rethink our engagement with issues of peace and conflict?

As I talk with my non-Quaker friends, it seems perhaps that Quakers as a body have a slightly worn image. Does the peace testimony mean anything real for us, now? Can we answer with any confidence the despairing off-the-cuff remark of Tony Blair on the eve of the Iraq invasion: 'It's all very well being a pacifist, but to be a pacifist after September 11, that is something different. It's all new now . . . '

And there are further, pressing questions: do we have something to say and do which is distinctive from the many others working alongside us for peace and justice? Is there a specifically Quaker dimension which adds anything to a secular/political analysis with which we might concur?

Before addressing these questions we need to look at the 'big picture', the wider context in which this rethinking is taking place. In the next chapter, therefore, we will look more closely at the global society of which we are a part and at the issues it raises for us. I hope this will give us a clearer sense of where, and how, to begin to frame our responses.

2

Facing the dilemmas

And when they ask us
And they're certainly going to ask us
The reason why we didn't win the croix de guerre
We'll never tell them, oh we'll never tell them
There was a front, but
Damned if we knew where.

Oh! What a Lovely War (Theatre Workshop, 1963)

World society is a system

One of the factors contributing to the rethink by Quakers of our peace witness is the rapid and unpredictable way human society is changing. It is worth briefly looking at this afresh, familiar though some of the facts may be.

We are citizens in the global village. We have one food supply, one set of common problems, despite efforts by governments, media and others to convince us otherwise. Through developments in communication, trade and transport, we are all in actual or potential contact with each other, strangers and friends alike. We cannot ignore each other any more. We are truly interdependent.

So, world society exists, here in my own house, not safely out there. The clothes I wear, the food and drink I consume, the radio and television programmes I like, the car I drive, the phones I use, the computer . . . All of them are made in other parts of world, as well as locally, by people from an unimaginable range of countries and cultures.

The system is faulty

The trouble is: the system is not working. Or rather it is working for some, in the short term, at the expense of the many and the long-term. In the UK living standards have been rising by 5% each year for the past 25 years (Crafts, 2002). Globally the proportion living in poverty has dropped from 24% in 1990 to 20% today. In East Asia improvements, at least for a substantial part of the population, have been dramatic.

But Africa has remained static or fallen back: in 1960 Senegal and South Korea had an average annual income per head of $230. By 2000 South Korea's average had increased to $8,910, while Senegal's was just $260. The world's richest country, Switzerland, has a per capita income nearly 80 times higher than in the world's poorest region, South Asia.

The divisions in world society have become wider. We now use a variety of phrases to describe the difference between the have-lots and the have-less. Majority and minority worlds is one delineation. Global South and Global North is another; two-thirds world, one-thirds world is another. Each refers not primarily to any geographical concepts. Rather they refer to interlocking populations, found on the same land mass. Those with the preponderance of power and wealth in all countries are contrasted with the usually larger group of marginalised and often powerless people. The smaller, minority world has its core financial and political centres in the 'North' and 'West', but it has outposts in nearly every country: at government level, in the security sector and in business especially, where elites keep minority interests dominant, while the majority world has its representatives in all major urban centres, and often in outlying rural areas too. Members of the Society of Friends are of course split, as is the world population as a whole, the greater proportion being members of the majority world.

Of cows and people

Poverty for the 'two-thirds world' is grinding and unrelenting. One billion people get less than $1 per day. Four billion people, two-thirds of the world's population, live on less than $2 a day (United Nations, 2002). *The average European cow, which receives a $2.20 per day subsidy from the taxpayer, is better provided for than a majority of the world's population.*

The poorest country in the UN index, Sierra Leone, enjoys a

standard of living typical in Europe 600 years ago. People in Britain live on average 30 years longer than in Africa, as AIDS, TB and malaria attack 300 million people in Asia and Africa each year, and directly kill 6.5 million of these. A woman dies in childbirth every minute.

The cost to the environment is also dire, with water running short, and global warming leading to rising sea levels. The number of people injured or made homeless by resultant natural disasters has risen from 740 million in the 1970s to more than 2 billion in the 1990s. Every dollar invested in Bangladesh now is absorbed by the cost of dealing with predictable disasters. And this is causing widespread migration: environmental refugees now outnumber political refugees by 25 million to 12. Further rises in sea levels will exacerbate this relentlessly.

Meantime some one million people each year died from armed conflict in the last half of the twentieth century. And the figures are not showing any improvement.

It can't go on like this

If we go on as we are the system will run into the sand. The World Bank envisages a world of nine billion people by 2050, with an economy four times what it is now. That would reduce poverty to a great extent but the Bank itself says that the price would be environmental catastrophe, increased conflict and social breakdown. Violence, poverty and environmental degradation are inextricably linked, together, and to our survival. Our children's future is being endangered, let alone that of our grandchildren.

We know much of all this, from personal experience as well as the media. And yet we – at least most of us – continue to lead our lives as if indeed there will always be a tomorrow like today. And, in doing so, we make things even worse.

I am sipping a comforting cup of hot coffee in my favourite café in town. At £1.75 this feels pricey. It feels worse when I learn that the farmer receives only 1.5p of that. Coffee farmers receive half as much as they did a decade ago. The coffee industry is worth twice as much as in 1990. I visited Nyeri, a coffee growing area in Kenya in 2002. There had been violence between the growers as they fought against declining prices for their coffee, and reducing incomes. They had decided to organise and fight back, but their power is small, as yet. Meanwhile their standard of living is desperate.

My mobile phone exemplifies another aspect of the world in my pocket. It is made with a mineral, coltan, that is found in very few places. To get it companies buy from traders in the Democratic Republic of Congo, in Central Africa. The trade is highly lucrative and, in the often chaotic conditions of Congo, the struggle to control it is a major cause of violence. When I buy a mobile I am buying into that situation, more or less unaware. Violent conflict is being fed by my habits.

When I drive to a Quaker meeting for worship in my car I know it is bad for the environment, but it doesn't seem to affect anyone directly. But each time I do that I confirm my membership of the car-dependent-culture which is fuelling the efforts to control the remaining sources of oil in the world. Would there have been such a push to invade Iraq if it did not house 25% of the world's oil reserves, while the US, UK and other large economies depend on oil as an alcoholic craves drink? And that ignores the climatic effects.

Changing conflicts
The faults in the system are also promoting violent conflict
When differences cannot be settled peacefully, it seems to many in the majority world that self-appointed elders in the global village – the USA and its allies, including Britain and usually the EU, in the present world order – have developed the simple technique of appropriating resources to themselves as they feel fit and rewriting the rules of trade and international finance to suit their economic and political interests. All in the name of democracy and freedom. Where there is dissent, it seems to people in the majority world that countries are pressurised through the threatened withholding of benefits and aid, or allocated extra inducements, or they use their armies, or local militias to do the job for them. If this account of contrasting perceptions seems harsh, we can notice that it is the global system which is deemed to work this way – despite the participation in it of fine people with high values.

With all this intense instability and injustice violent conflicts are virtually inevitable.

Since the collapse of the Soviet Union in 1989 these have increasingly been internal, between groups operating within a particular state, rather than between states. Wars formerly fought between the standing armies of states are more often fought by rival militias of shifting allegiance, or between militias and governments. The spoils are to do with power and control of minerals as much as over territory itself, backed by vested interests heavily involved in the drugs or arms trades. Civil populations, no longer bystanders, have themselves become targets and their destruction a means of instilling terror and control, a throwback to the time of the Hundred Years War in Europe.

The large numbers of people seeking asylum are a result of this social and political breakdown. An asylum seeker comes from another part of the global village. She is not a foreigner, disconnected and desperate. She is suffering the results of the same village administration system of which I am part. If my part 'works' and hers doesn't, it needs to be fixed, or we all suffer. The curious thing is that even those areas which seem to do well out of the system, in terms of wealth for example, do not seem happy. They often have high suicide rates, and many are alienated from their own families and communities.

Peacemakers have to choose whose vision they are promoting

Whatever the causes, all wars are now essentially between 'us': either within, or between countries, they are all within the same system. Every war is a civil war, and reflects deep failures of the global system.

There is a concomitant loss of orientation here, of faith, of genuine spirituality which poses questions for us as Quakers: do we have anything to offer, or are we, lacking faith and conviction ourselves, simply caught up and neutralised? Each of us is potentially cause and effect. Each of us is also potentially a healer, a peacemaker.

And all of us concerned to find a way to build true wellbeing and peace are challenged to choose: to identify our own path and to work strategically. To work for human wellbeing at all levels – for a system which is geared to meeting common needs in an environmentally sustainable way on a global level – may seem to be fairly tame and obvious. It might have been ten years ago. Now it is antithetical to the dominant minority world paradigm, of which our own country is a *de facto* supporter.

Making a choice to stand against this paradigm could make us rebels in the face of political changes at home and attract a price tag beyond that which most of us have become accustomed to. 'Nice' people would have to get rather harder, rather sharper, rather tougher.

War on whose terror?

The starkness of the choice facing us has become clearer since the events of September 11 in New York and October 7, when Afghanistan was attacked. Subsequent events in Iraq and elsewhere have emphasised further the fractured state of world society. As the 'war on terror' has subsequently gathered pace, so it has become obvious that a consensus view of global violence and other problems – glimpsed albeit briefly when the Berlin Wall came down in 1989 and there was talk of a global peace dividend – was disappearing at the same speed. Some see terrorists as governments intent on enforcing their will on others, using whatever means necessary. Others see terrorists as small groups operating out of a flat in London or Milan. Peace is a highly contested term.

The minority world view, set out trenchantly in Washington and proclaimed boldly by the Project for a New American Century (see www.newamericancentury.org), holds that any threat to US security constitutes a threat to world security and peace. US rule is the only practical way to reestablish world peace. 'The international environment is far more likely to enjoy peace under a single hegemon. Moreover, we are not just any hegemon. We run a uniquely benign imperium' is a comment from an insider. The phrase often used is 'total spectrum domination'. The US defence budget now allocates $1 billion per day to defence, and the figure is rising. This view goes together with a seeming inability in business and political circles to countenance the possibility that there might be any legitimate alternative to this worldview.

In Britain a proportion, though not the whole, of the political elite seems largely to accept this view, and has produced its own justifications of the 'new imperialism' as the only viable way of maintaining world order. Security is defined, to general agreement, as national security, which has to be protected at all costs. Pre-emption is now an official doctrine, tried and tested most recently in Iraq. The argument goes: 'if we perceive that a country or group might attack us, we will attack them first. And we are justified in doing so. As we embody the "good", we do not countenance that others could ever do this to us with any justification.'

Away from these centres, in the majority world, peace and the path to it is seen very differently. Amongst myriad views, there is often strong opposition to what is seen as western, Christian dominance, and a quite different idea of what constitutes security. Hostility is expressed towards apparent double standards, whereby, for example, Iraq was penalised for failing to comply with UN resolutions, and Israel is not. Calls are made to address the roots of terrorism, which lie in the malfunctioning of the world system, as a complement to dealing with its violent manifestations. Some of the major current wars (those in Chechnya and Palestine-Israel for example) are seen primarily as about social justice, not terrorism. Strong voices are heard denouncing the ever growing inequalities in international wealth and expounding the view that the rich North bears the main responsibility for global pollution and climate change.

In this alternative space, civil society organisations such as trade unions, peasant associations, religious institutions, human rights and development organisations, media and community groups and relief agencies are all playing roles. In this developing view, a strong civil society, independent of government, is essential if countries are to be able to address their own internal conflicts effectively.

Different assumptions, different solutions

Not surprisingly, these divergent views of how the world should be lead to radically different approaches to resolving conflict. On the one side the issue appears to be seen as largely one of disorder, giving rise to the largely straightforward need, in principle at least, to acquire the necessary resources in order to maintain the current world order, using whatever force is necessary.

On the other, as I know at first hand from the many practitioners who have attended RTC courses, there is a vast array of creative energy to address conflicts: those which arise from local struggles for social justice and an equitable access to resources as well as those arising from global clashes of power and influence. Grave conflicts can be seen as opportunities to generate new, more secure futures for people and states, and a chance to develop new, nonviolent ways to deal with interstate conflicts – as well as enhance existing ones. Conflict transformation, in such contexts as this, can and does involve a whole range of activities, some not usually associated with 'peace' work. Divergent thinking demands that one looks behind the presenting issues, and to the long term.

In the case of Iraq, for example, this view would suggest that we needed, and still need as part of the long term problem, to address the global overdependence on oil. To do so we should call into question the whole car culture. Options open to us, which were all publicly advocated before the invasion, include: reclaiming the streets by direct action, promoting walking and cycling, strengthening public transport, opposing new road construction, paying the full cost of car use, promoting renewable fuels, educating the public, arguing for land-use policies which reduce the need for car travel. Quakers might want to develop a new testimony against the car.

The essence of effective conflict transformation, as we shall see later in this lecture, is creativity, and diverse cooperation through networks. In the case of Iraq, the global movement started to prevent the invasion has become the most extensive network to prevent war that there has ever been.

If not now, when, if not me, who?
The story of the boiled frog is chilling. A frog which is dropped into a pot of boiling water will apparently jump out immediately (though I have admittedly not tried this). If however it is placed in a saucepan of cold water, it will remain while the water is slowly heated to boiling point and die. It never gets the message that it needs to jump out. Its systems are designed to deal with instant, rather than gradual, danger.

Our frontline, our point of entry into this situation, is, it seems to me, here and it is now. We have literally to *re-cognise* it, to become consciously and explicitly aware of it, wherever we are. In doing so we will find, in the coming chapters, that we can usefully learn from others who are treading the same path in different settings. They can enable us to act more intelligently, and coherently.

SIGNPOSTS

In Chapters 1 and 2, as we begin our search to interpret afresh our peace witness for today, we have taken time to revisit some of the historic values and testimonies of the Religious Society of Friends. We have set them in the context of some of the courageous work Quakers have undertaken down the centuries, and are still doing, and within the wider, secular framework of world society. This we have seen, and know from our experience, poses a deep challenge to our witness and to our integrity. In early times Quakers could, for the most part, see clearly the points at which the requirements of the law and the ways of the world contravened what was right, and what genuine Christianity demanded. In these cases they resisted, sometimes at great cost to themselves.

Today these points are less clear. Our testimonies to peace and equality are being compromised each day: each of us plays our role in the global system, as consumer and producer. Wars are fought, invasions undertaken with our resources, however reluctantly. We feel guilty, but do not know how to free ourselves.

However, there are many encouraging developments. We are very far from alone in our quest for right living, for justice and peace. People of many countries, persuasions and religions are our companions.

I want to introduce you in the next chapter to several of these people. I can write about them because I have been lucky enough to work alongside them for a good number of years. In meeting them we will also learn something of the distinctive way in which they try to make sense of, and deal with, conflict and injustice.

In subsequent chapters the encounter with these people, and their knowledge and experience, will be brought together with our own

Quaker history and purpose to help us in the search for a fresh sense
of what our peace witness entails today, rooted in reality and our experience of the Spirit at work in humankind.

A dream?

Let's allow ourselves to dream for a moment. Imagine that the
world's leaders wake up to the self-evident fact that their security
cannot any longer be guaranteed by national frontiers. Instead they
realise that their security depends on the security of everyone. The
US government, with by far the largest defence budget, decides to
take a lead and allocate its defence budget, for one year only in the
first instance, to building security. What does it do?

With the $360 billion available, it finds it is able to provide:

- Basic health and nutrition for everyone
- Reproductive health for all women
- Universal education
- Clean water and healthy sewage systems for all
- Access to energy for all over 20 years old
- Debt relief for the 33 most indebted countries.

- $12 billion could be allocated to fighting AIDS, TB and malaria, and
- $17 billion would be available for investing in nonviolent peace-
  keeping.
  (figures from *Observer*, August 2002)

Britain's defence budget is about one tenth of this, but the possibilities are still enormous, when we wake up.

3

Lives that speak

Welfare or politics: whose game are we playing?

The threats to human survival can seem daunting to all of us. Carrying a 'peace and justice' label as I inevitably do, people in this country often ask me: how do you keep going? What gives you hope? It is a question for all of us, for out of our answer, deeply pondered, may come a new sense of energy and direction.

The question I frequently want to ask in reply to many of my friends in Britain, is 'Why is this just my problem? How do you manage to lead your lives as if the problems of the wider world are not your business?' I do not mean by this that such people are not compassionate. They are often very kind and generous, giving freely to charities, for example. They sometimes have jobs in the caring professions and are active church members. But essentially these are people who accept the current arrangements of human affairs as given, out of their control and influence; their giving seeks to mitigate its worst, and by implication, inevitable effects. They adopt what one might term a welfare approach to human issues.

This is understandable, but, I think, flawed. Why? Fundamentally because it is based on denial. Denial of the fact that we are each of us, everyday, active players in human society, local and global. Our choices of how we use our time, energy and resources demonstrate which side of the fence we are on (majority or minority world?) every bit as much as how we spend our money and which church or mosque we go to. They demonstrate what our politics are in the face of social injustice: we either accept the situation, and perhaps try to mitigate the effects through charity, or we go the extra mile and adopt an essentially political approach. Accepting our inescapable part in the way the world works, and the fact that for many of us British Quakers a relatively free country gives us two incomparable advantages – freedom to be politically active and freedom from the danger of hunger – we look for ways to address the very rules of the game, which decide who gains and who loses.

There was a film recently advertised in Birmingham whose catch-phrase ran: 'It's not how you play the game, but how the game plays you.' The game, as we have seen in Chapter 2, is loaded against the many in favour of the few. It is as if we are playing a football match in which one side, though many fewer in number than the other side, has the right to a special quota of free kicks and can play for half an hour longer. As long as we lead our lives uncritical of the order of things around us, and unengaged in some way in trying to make those rules more inclusive and more just, the game is playing us.

Being more strategic

For Friends there has always been a powerful symbiosis between our worship and our witness in the world. We pride ourselves on the fact that our commitment is to 'that of God in everyone'. But I wonder if we have yet fully understood what it means to be political, to challenge the rules of the game. Sometimes it seems to me that our theory of change consists in something like the following: our witness, born out of concern, will lead increasingly to change in other individuals, until eventually the desired wider change takes place. We look back at prominent individuals in our past, such as Margaret Fell and Elizabeth Fry, and see them as luminaries who, by their example, changed the way things were done. In fact they were arguably able to bring change because they had a certain position in society, and were able to use it, and their gender, strategically.

The question I am posing here is: how can we, as Quakers, be more strategic in our pursuit of our testimonies for peace and equality? Do we know how we would like to see change happen, as well as where we want to go?

Inner Light

Pondering this question brings to mind the response to a similar, apoc-ryphal question supposedly put to a peasant in Ireland: when asked 'How do I get to Limerick?' his answer was 'Don't start from here.' For us, as Quakers, the answer is surely the opposite: 'Start here.' Indeed

'Stand here' would be a better beginning: 'Stand in the Light'. Most of us would relate this favourite phrase to what we call the 'inner Light', the Christ within, the Inward Teacher. It is Quaker language for the transforming power of God's light, which can and does illuminate and transform us, if we will allow it. None of us, I think, would doubt that going inward, opening the 'eye of the heart' as the mystics have frequently put it, in whatever way is authentic for each person, is fundamental work, a crucial element in living our truth in the world. We shall look at that more closely in Chapter 7.

Outer Light

There is however also a sense in which, if we are to challenge violence as wisely and fully as our history and capacity indicate we can, and build alternatives, we need to be fully open to the external, growing light of knowledge and experience of social change and conflict transformation. What light can we find out there?

The political landscape just now is obscure. With a few exceptions many political leaders, in Britain as elsewhere, find themselves in a vortex from which they cannot free themselves without huge cost.

We are fortunate however, that our globalised society has also given rise to countervailing influences to the sometimes suffocating system we experience. Since the end of the second world war, and arguably earlier, insights have been accumulating as scholars, politicians, religious leaders and practitioners alike have put their minds and their hearts into avoiding war and building lasting peace.

In the UK alone there are now some fifty institutes and non-governmental organisations dedicated to the study and practice of conflict transformation. While British Quakers are well represented both as academics and practitioners, it seems sometimes as if Britain Yearly Meeting has, over the past ten to fifteen years, kept itself aloof institutionally from too close an involvement with developments in this field. As these innovations have taken place, there is a sense in which the Society has remained a well-meaning, slightly reluctant amateur in a burgeoning, perhaps rather more 'professional' community working for peace and justice.

Interestingly this detached attitude of the Society to social causes seems to have been typical in the nineteenth and twentieth centuries: temperance, slavery, suffrage, to name a few, were taken up by influential, activist Friends while the Yearly Meeting prevaricated in the face of its own disunity and the contentious issue of whether a religious body should concern itself with politics.

Practitioners speak

We are going now to take a closer look at this wider community, to get a sense of who belongs to it and what we might be able to learn from them.

You will meet below some of the many colleagues who have given me hope, and taught me much. They have faced enormous challenges in some of the world's most intractable conflicts and found energy and new hope. They are engaged people, faced with the range of competing demands we ourselves are familiar with, except that these demands are in some cases more directly, more immediately life threatening.

Introducing them briefly to you I hope you will get a sense of the courage and sheer life that is manifested in their lives and be infected with the hope which comes from living and working alongside ordinary people who will not take no for an answer, and who do not understand the words 'impossible' or 'give up'.

Imagine, in the room with you now, are six people, in equal numbers of men and women: Dekha from Northern Kenya, Ehsan from Afghanistan, Tanja from Serbia, Emma and Ngarm from Cambodia, Paul from Wales. There is warmth and laughter in the air as they talk. Sometimes a song or a joke. Sometimes a silence. Their conversation is reflective, sometimes sad. All have faced major challenges and have come through them, so far.

Dekha

Dekha is a Kenyan Somali in her mid thirties. A mother of four, she comes from Wajir, a remote town in the far north of Kenya, close to the border with Ethiopia and Somalia. Dressed traditionally, with a shawl draped over her head, Dekha looks every inch a traditional Somali woman. She was a teacher in a local school in the early 1990s when her town was rocked by violence caused by rival clans fighting. In an area of desperate poverty, neglected by governments over many years, the people were very vulnerable to provocation and misinformation. Dekha and several of her women colleagues saw their families suffering, both from the killings and the resultant dislocation of the nomadic lifestyle which most of the people depended on. Inspired by a passionate belief in Islam, a deep concern for life and their children, and energised by rising anger that such destruction could be wrought by their own, male-dominated leadership, they formed a group to address first of all the need to stop the killings.

Over a period of months, despite immense opposition and apathy, they managed to achieve this, and then to mobilise different sectors of the population including elders, local government, women, ex-combatants and youth. The groups were then brought together in a single coordinating peace group, set up to take responsibility for peace and security in the whole area. A prime function of the group was to ensure that people had access to adequate information, to counter the continuous danger of false information put about by those wishing to plunge the area back into violence and to provide a practical, nonpartisan means to prevent outbreaks of violence. They took their lobbying as far as the office of the President in Nairobi, where Dekha and her colleagues went to press the needs of their area on several occasions.

As stability returned the Peace Group evolved into the Peace and Development Committee, and developed a new capacity to work on long term underlying issues such as education (especially for pastoralists) and deprivation, as well as maintaining a continuing ability to deal with immediate situations through a rapid response team. Dekha herself has widened her focus now to address the wider regional and crossborder issues which continue to threaten instability in the whole area, including Wajir. (A video, *The Wajir Story*, has been produced as part of a series of African peacebuilding case studies.)

At the same time she has seen the importance of linking to others working on peace and justice issues elsewhere: local issues are always connected to wider influences, regional and beyond. She was a staff member of RTC for three years, and a lead tutor on many of its courses. She is a cofounder of the Coalition for Peace in Africa, a continent-wide network of practitioners. She combines her regional work with being a board member of Coexistence International, where global issues relevant to her area and others like it can be addressed. When in late 2002 a hotel was bombed in Mombasa where many Israelis were staying, Dekha led a group the next day to offer condolences on behalf of Kenyans. Kenyan police officers initially refused her permission to enter the hotel. Dekha, being persistent, stayed near the hotel with the friends. She then recognised a police officer whom she had worked with in Wajir and he, after discussion, allowed Dekha and her team inside. She seems to relish opposition, and gain energy and conviction from it. Above and beyond it all is a deep and unquestioning commitment to Islam as a practical way to live a life of struggle, peace and love.

Ehsan

Ehsan, on her left, is in his mid forties, already greying and thoughtful. Ehsan, like Dekha, is a devout Muslim. He was a guerilla during the occupation of Afghanistan by the Soviet Union in the 1980s, during which his brother was killed and his family fled as refugees across the border to Peshawar in Pakistan. When the occupation was over Afghanistan continued in a state of lawlessness and while some of his colleagues decided to continue under arms, for that was the 'trade' they had come to know best, Ehsan was moved by a vision and a passion for justice and peace which arose both from his deep commitment to Islam and from the loss in war of family members and friends: he has great reserves of determination, and is well versed in knowledge of Islam as a religion of peace and justice.

He, like Dekha, was well before his time. In his case he obtained a job with an international agency but lost it without notice when he made it clear that his priority was to build peace as well as feed the hungry. During a training course which he attended with RTC in 1993 he saw that without working specifically on the post-conflict issues of reconciliation and dialogue, and addressing other peace-related issues, the aid programmes flooding his country would lead to nothing but a continuation of violence. He conceived the idea of

mobilising fellow Afghan relief and development workers into a network for peacebuilding. It took some time, for peace at that time was
not thought to be a legitimate matter for aid agencies. However at the
individual level he found Afghan colleagues, initially mostly men (for
cultural reasons) but increasingly women also, eager to follow his lead.
The network took the name Cooperation for Peace and Unity (CPAU)
and rapidly developed its own programmes in specific provinces inside
Afghanistan. The focus was on rebuilding local methods of conflict
resolution, destroyed during the fighting, and training agency staff in
ways of analysing and dealing sensitively with the tensions and conflicts in the areas where they were working.

This work continued even as the Taliban made such initiatives
increasingly difficult. Once the US had removed the Taliban the network came under renewed pressure, this time because its members
and staff were prime candidates for places in the new government, in
the human rights and development sphere especially. It is a major
struggle now to maintain the network in the face of the pressures and
the urgency of so many tasks. Ehsan, like Dekha, has moved out of a
central role in CPAU to make room for others. He is now a government minister, responsible for setting up a hugely ambitious
programme of democratic renewal at village level entitled the National
Solidarity Programme. He has also been playing a key role in facilitating the national consultations leading up to a new constitution for
Afghanistan. As if that was not enough, a major additional challenge
for him now is his ministerial colleagues, as I discovered on a visit to
Kabul in 2003. Half the cabinet are, in his terms, warlords, including
the minister of defence, and many of them have kept their private
militias. As Ehsan put it to me: 'What sort of peace are they willing
to sign up for?'

Emma and Ngarm

Emma and Ngarm live in Phnom Penh, Cambodia. Ngarm is a
member of the Society of Friends, a Cambodian national and survivor
of the horrors of the Khmer Rouge, though his family suffered badly.
For ten years he served as a soldier in the resistance to the Viet-
namese occupation of Cambodia, before deserting when he became

disillusioned with the way the struggle was being waged. Shortly afterwards he helped to establish Cambodia's first conflict resolution centre and was a pioneer trainer for conflict resolution training in the country. He has an MA in Peace Studies from Bradford University and is a deep thinker who often wears a quizzical look. He is puzzling over how Cambodia, and the wider region, are going to overcome the legacy of war, and his work is on practical aspects of reconciliation and rebuilding society. Emma is from Australia, a former worker with the World Council of Churches and still active on its international committees. She moved to live in Cambodia when she married Ngarm two years ago. Her inspiration is deeply Christian, but not exclusively so. It finds its expression in a profound empathy for, and solidarity with, others, especially the casualties of life.

An activist to her fingertips, Emma has worked in many parts of the world including East Timor, and specialises in the peace-related issues of South Asia. They are both at the hub of Action Asia, part of a global network called ACTION for Conflict Transformation. They are working to build up the numbers and capacity of those working for peace and justice in the region. They take an active part in visits by the network to Burma (Myanmar), and have conducted a workshop on conflict transformation there, which most informed people had thought was impossible.

Tanja

Tanja is a Serb, living now in Belgrade. Originally a teacher from Kosovo, she had to flee with her family when the NATO bombs started falling. It is not a realistic option for her to return, given the open hostility existing between the few remaining Serbs and the majority Albanian population in the province. She, like several others in this room, has turned the fact and the grief of being a casualty of war into an engine for empowerment. I first met her when she had just escaped from Kosovo: her eyes seemed irrevocably sunk in the purple-grey bags below them and her pain and melancholy were written all over her face. Now she still has trouble letting go, relaxing. We joke with her about the stern look she carries and urge her to smile, which she does with good grace, and lights up her face as she does so.

Tanja has no formal religion, perhaps partly because in Serbia much formal religion is the home of the political right. But she has a quiet and uncompromising love for her colleagues, and an iron determination to resist the next bout of revenge which her people could be led into if the political process in Serbia falters. She is part of a small and highly dynamic team working to rebuild dialogue and understanding between the different communities living in Serbia. They focus on three main constituencies: students in their twenties, young politicians and members of political youth groups, and journalists. This team, in turn, is part of a wider project, funded by the Norwegian government. There are eight teams working across former Yugoslavia on similar issues, aiming to rebuild communication and reduce prejudice and discrimination.

Increasingly they see this work as building the foundations for accountable democracy and greater social justice in the face of widespread corruption and a loss of hope, as evidenced by the emigration of many young people. Now she and her colleagues are cautiously hopeful that the cycle of violence can be stopped and that things can be different, even though she may never be able to go home. They have yet, however, to solve the problem of chronic overwork and exhaustion.

Paul

Paul, like those we met above, is an enabler as well as a doer. Living in Wales, he is Jewish by background: two of his grandparents fled from Russia and escaped the pogroms. He made a visit to Israel in his early twenties, which left him indignant and angry at the treatment of Palestinians and convinced him that he could never share the political identity of his relatives. He seems to have transmuted this anger into a passion for showing the world that humankind must move on: there are infinitely better ways to deal with conflicts than to reject, to maim and to kill. These habitual ways will only perpetuate misery. His background is in counselling, mediation and training, and during the 1990s he worked with asylum seekers and in race relations, and, amongst much else, set up a community mediation scheme in Milton Keynes, where he lived.

During the mid nineties he came to realise that his life was a little too predictable: he needed to take risks, to find new challenges, if he was to continue to develop as a person and to be true to his values. He began to search for ways of making his work touch on the wider global situation. He realised that to be free to do that, which would probably necessitate being free to travel at short notice, he would have to give up his regular work commitments. So, without any fanfare, but with a quiet word in my ear, he took the risk, with his partner, and made space for new things to happen. They did.

For some ten years Paul has contributed his skills in mediation and negotiation in many places outside the UK: the Balkans, the Caucasus, Russia, Kazakhstan, the Philippines, Nigeria, Sierra Leone, Sudan, Cameroun . . . the list goes on. He has been active in promoting ACTION wherever he goes. He is freelance, but has avoided making money the focus. He will do substantial work for nothing, if necessary. And he has still continued to work in the UK, as a trainer for community facilitators and an adviser for the government's Neighbourhood Renewal Unit. In his 'spare' time he is involved in local community affairs, and took an active role in the campaign against the invasion of Iraq.

Now, as you ask him, he tells you he feels in danger of burnout, and somewhat isolated despite the international contacts he has. Freelancing brings rewards of independence and freedom to choose, but it also can be a lonely road, and serves to emphasise the importance of solidarity with, and support for, each other in this struggle.

Ordinary yet prophetic

What makes this small group special? In one sense, not much really. They are rather typical of a much wider group, ordinary people who have seen the challenges which serious peacebuilding poses. Some were born into instability and war and responded, others found themselves in a relatively peaceful environment and came to see that their comfort was indivisible from the instability and oppression elsewhere in the world. All took risks to be doing what they are, far above what they needed to do to survive.

Beyond that we can perhaps distinguish three processes at work, which have the potential to speak to us as Quakers also.

A crucial first step for each member of this group was to stop, to look afresh at their own circumstances, and to recognise their responsibility for whatever was taking place. They became aware that they were political actors, whether they chose to play this role actively or not. As part of this process they came to address their own inner voices, laid down deeply in their minds as part of their biography, wider history and culture. These voices, or assumptions, are sometimes termed, collectively, as internalised oppression. They can often speak silently of submission, fatalism, despair: 'we can do nothing' – especially in situations of prolonged deprivation or violent conflict. Once we name them, and articulate them, they can lose their power, and we cease to be victims of our situation. In that process energies are freed up and we find ourselves empowered to act.

It is not coincidental that all have a spiritual approach to life. Not that they would agree for a moment on how to describe it. Amongst them can be found followers of Islam, Christianity, Buddhism and their own unlabelled light. But this process of personal and political self-discovery, of 'conscientisation', as Paulo Freire the Brazilian educator put it, almost necessarily awakens in us an awareness of spirit. And spirit is clearly present in all they do, though none of them feels the need to claim exclusive insights to the truth.

A second step they have taken is to make a decision to stand out against the injustices which they saw being perpetrated around them. They have sought ways of living out alternatives to the violence and win/lose models of problem solving they observed and experienced.

Thirdly, as they have done this, they have also decided to go beyond being 'not violent': to promote actively nonviolent approaches to oppression and violence in all its manifestations – even though they might not, being argumentative souls, all accept the term nonviolence as applying to them. For some this decision has come from a religious conviction. For others, it has emerged from experiencing the devastation and horror that violence brings. Either way it has entailed adopting a strategic, long-term approach to change.

And now they are models for others, prophets in some sense, pointing up contradictions as they see them and embodying – not just talking about – a different future.

Contradictions: who is peace for?

One crucial contradiction they are wrestling with is: who benefits from this peace we are struggling for? Who is preventing us from building it? The threat they see is not primarily Al Qaida, or other international terrorist groups. These are symptoms, albeit alarming ones. The main threat they see is a rampant global disorder, characterised by widening inequalities of wealth and power, and the apparently growing use of open violence by a number of states, including the most militarily powerful nation on earth. In this disorder they have seen peace in many areas becoming synonymous with pacification, a state in which there is enforced stability and compliance with global economic and political interests, housed in the minority world. They are, in response, struggling to reassert and recreate an inclusive peace, owned and protected by the people who live in it, free of external domination. Empowerment is a word they often use, albeit self-critically, for that is seen as a jargon word which risks being as meaningless as the word 'sustainable' (another term in this field) has become.

Local and global

One further characteristic we can note is that this group of colleagues works both locally and globally, independently and together. The work of each is rooted strongly in the needs of the area in which they live and yet they pursue the issues which affect those communities beyond the local and national boundaries to the international level. Often this is by mail, encouraging each other, or by lobbying and campaigning from where they are. Sometimes they need to travel. Emma visited Dekha to work with the Wajir community on landmines education. Paul has worked with Tanja and her team on the education of future political leaders in Serbia. Dekha has assisted with both development education and community work in the UK. They recently completed work, with others in the ACTION network, on preparing a book setting out some of their insights into peacebuilding arising from recent experience.

And this cooperation is not by chance; it is part of the commitment that a growing number of people in this field have to each other, a commitment that is growing as the size and nature of the threat becomes clear. Here, in short, we find a global community of resistance, which goes under many names: a community that works to its own value-based priorities and prioritises relationships and social justice. We shall return to this theme later in the book.

Their membership of ACTION helps to sustain their momentum. This network, initiated and initially resourced by RTC and now independent, has in its four years of existence provided training on a self-help basis for its members in different aspects of peace and development work. Its source book, recently published, contains a digest of the wisdom generated over the past four years, and deals with themes such as: mobilising for change, intervening in conflict, advocacy and influencing, training and learning. It is a resource for fellow practitioners, part of the action-research which characterises much peace work today.

The diagram opposite was developed by ACTION members to establish their values and vision. The intention was to set out what unites the members. But it was also to make clear the differences which exist between them, on the one hand, and other organisations and networks whose concept of peace is rather different.

Differing values

Why is this question of values important to us as Quakers involved in peace work? Because, as we engage more courageously and strategically with peace and justice issues – even at some risk perhaps to ourselves – it is increasingly important to know who shares our analysis, and who our allies are.

To the outside, non-conflict-specialist world, one organisation which describes itself as working for conflict resolution or transformation is much the same in outlook as any other. In reality, the differences between them are stark: they cover the political spectrum, from right to left. They take their agendas from their funders, and their context, as well as their beliefs. They vary hugely in their approach to change.

There are those who know the precise nature of the change they want to bring, and the precise method they will use to get there.

Conflict Transformation is a holistic and multifaceted process of engaging with conflict. It aims to reduce violence and to protect and promote social justice and sustainable peace. It requires work in all spheres, at all levels and with all stakeholders.

Conflict Transformation needs to be accountable to those directly affected by conflict but requires networks and linkages to sustain it. Conflict Transformation is an ongoing process of changing relationships, behaviours, attitudes and structures, from the negative to the positive. It requires timely interventions, respect for cultural context, patience and persistence and a comprehensive understanding of specific conflicts.

As conflict is dynamic and Conflict Transformation is an ongoing process, learning is a vital component.

Most importantly, it begins with ourselves.

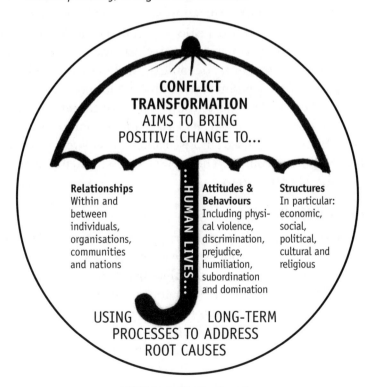

©ACTION for Conflict Transformation

They tend to have a more monocultural, rather than crosscultural, view of the world, and often to avoid being explicit about their values. This is partly, perhaps, because they tend to assume that everyone shares their view of the world, and partly because they know that to be explicit would involve them in a lively dialogue with others in the field, which they may not relish. These, 'value-free' organisations, are nearly all based in the global North.

At the other end of the spectrum are those who like to be more explicit about their values, including a strong commitment to cross-cultural exchange and sensitivity, but are completely open about what the outcome of any intervention will be in a specific situation, and how to get there.

At one pole, there are organisations which, before starting to work on new ideas and strategies, will take whole days of a seminar to elicit from participants how they see the world and the differences within it in order to build up, rather than impose, a common understanding of key concepts such as peace, justice and conflict. At the other pole there are organisations which teach precisely the same method to everyone, regardless of culture or context, much as a cook follows a recipe. I spoke once to a prominent North American former diplomat who had just been to Moscow to conduct a peace education seminar with primary school teachers. When I asked him what he expected the teachers to do next he looked surprised and replied: 'Well, teach it on Monday morning of course!' The 'it' was a step-by-step programme developed for schools in Iowa.

Critical peacebuilding

The contrasts between the two polarities are beginning to be recognised as substantial, with those whose work accentuates social justice and political change tending to describe their field as *critical* peacebuilding. This highlights a further point of distinction between the adherents of critical peacebuilding and those more in the mainstream: critical peacebuilding is holistic. It includes, as part of the problem to be addressed, the person or organisation doing the analysis, the intervenor, and their country of origin. This contrasts with the norm in the mainstream of the field, which is to treat a conflict as a localised phenomenon confined to the place where it is manifesting itself. In the mainstream, wider international structures and influences on local conflicts tend to be ignored. Politics is never far away in conflict work, beginning with analysis and ending in action.

Critical peacebuilding, therefore, calls into question the roles of international actors, of the 'North' and the 'South', and of the conflict transformation institutions themselves. Increasingly too, critical peacebuilding questions the way in which much, though far from all, of the theoretical knowledge we have accumulated about peace and conflict has tended to be created and driven in the global North, and raises queries, in the spirit of crosscultural cooperation and empowerment, about the cultural and political assumptions which are attached to it.

The political implications are obvious. If I analyse the conflict over Iraq, for example, by feeding in information relevant only to its apparent determination to develop and maintain the capacity to produce weapons of mass destruction, I will get a very different picture to the one I get when I include, for example, the history of how those weapons were sold to Iraq by international third parties, the global strategy of the United States government and the importance of oil to the industrialised economies. From these different pictures I am likely to arrive at quite different decisions about the nature of the problem, and how to address it.

The people we have encountered here could all be described as belonging to the critical peacebuilding camp, though being very practical people, most would not greatly value that terminology. They do provide some flavour of the creativity and commitment to nonviolent change which is emerging with renewed vigour across the world, and perhaps offer some food for thought about our own individual and institutional responses.

Since 1990 there has been a remarkable growth worldwide of organisations started to support and service this reinvigorated community of peace and justice workers. In the UK a number of nongovernmental organisations have taken up important roles in different parts of the field: in addition to Responding to Conflict (RTC), Conciliation Resources, International Alert, Oxford Research Group

and Safer World are amongst the most active and innovative of those
focusing substantially on conflict transformation. These agencies
form a more or less coherent community which coordinates activities and works together quite remarkably on many issues.

Quaker Peace and Social Witness is also active, staffed and supported by some excellent people. However, in the light of the salience
of violent conflict during the 1990s, the apparent decline in capacity
and ambition of the international arm of Britain Yearly Meeting has
been striking and, in the light of our history, it seems fair to raise questions about what, if anything, can be learned from this for the future.
We shall look at the challenges this raises in a little more depth later
in this book.

SIGNPOSTS

At this point, however, having got to know a little about some practitioners of conflict transformation, and observed some aspects which
we might learn from, we are going to find out more about how such
people – and their many colleagues, including Responding to Conflict
itself – plan and act. How do they, often in the midst of turbulent conditions, decide what they should do, and how to do it? We have
together developed and elaborated some useful frameworks and
understandings. These frameworks have the potential also to help
Quakers see our own options more clearly. In the next few pages we
look briefly at three basic ideas: conflict, violence and peace. As we
unpick each idea, and put it together again, we may simultaneously
find new thinking coming to us which we can apply to our own quest
for rethinking our peace witness, here and now.

4

Making sense of violence and peace

An innocent observer might be excused for thinking that terms such as conflict prevention, conflict resolution, conflict reduction, conflict mitigation, conflict transformation give a strong clue that conflict is the core problem which peace work is designed to address. In practice, this is not so. At least not for many, and perhaps especially not for those we encountered in the last chapter, who are working from a critical peacebuilding perspective. For them conflict is not a problem in itself. They see conflict as quite distinct from violence, as an everyday phenomenon which is an integral element of any organisation or society and necessary for social and political change. The key problem for them is not conflict but violence. A deep analysis of violence can clarify what we mean by peace, and enable us to see the potential role of conflict in the struggle for peace and justice.

What do we mean by violence?

Violent behaviour takes place at all levels of all societies, as far as we know, from within the home to state and then international level. We are made continuously aware of it, most of us more by the media than by our own experience. War, murder, maiming, intimidation and the many other aspects of violent behaviour, presented in isolated and random-seeming chunks, can be enormously discouraging and disempowering. Friends have often sought to address this 'direct' violence through mediation and 'good offices'.

But we know that there is much more to violence than meets the eye or hits the headlines. When we are close to such violence ourselves, in our homes or our neighbourhoods, and have first hand knowledge of it we can see that it has roots. It can be explained. 'Mindless violence', however it may seem on the outside, usually means 'violence that I cannot understand, or that the perpetrators do not wish to explain'.

In the search for the roots of violent behaviour, one of the crucial early insights of peace studies was that people can be damaged as much by underlying, often almost invisible, structures as by the behaviour itself. Any one of the estimated one million people to have died in Iraq during the 1990s as a result of shortages of food and medicines could have testified to the purely abstract difference between death as a result of sanctions, a legal structure of prohibition, and death as a result of a bullet. On a less extreme and more local scale, women who meet the 'glass ceiling' and cannot get the top jobs, or black people who cannot get promotion on merit in the Metropolitan Police are encountering essentially similar structures.

Violence consists of structures, visible and invisible

An example may help to clarify this idea of structure. A Congolese colleague and his wife, hospital technicians who worked as mediators and peace campaigners for many years in their remote home area of Bunia in northeastern Congo, described to me the killings of hundreds of people in all its horror. When asked the reasons for the atrocities, despite all their work, their observations were matter of fact: a low level and long contained hostility between the Hema and the Ngiti people was deliberately stoked up by a small number of traders in gold and coltan (needed for mobile phones as we saw earlier in the book), both of which are mined in the area. If there was law and order, the traders would have to pay taxes. In the disorder they could make off with all the highly lucrative proceeds. Surely the presence of Ugandan troops should help to restore order? Well, no. They are in fact actively provoking further violence, by spreading false information, for example. In that way they can justify their continued presence (to keep order) and profit from the mineral trade in their turn.

Underlying the violence, described if at all in the Western press in terms such as 'age-old inter-ethnic rivalries' there is therefore a *structure*, a *context* already given in the area: a history of containable hostility, the absence of legitimate government and law enforcement, the presence of Ugandan troops, the lucrative trade in minerals, the presence of traders.

But there is another, deeper dimension which also plays its part:

the internal, invisible area of attitudes, beliefs, values and culture. These are not violent in themselves, but can easily promote violent behaviour and allow violent structures to persist unchallenged. In the context of Congo we would include here the continuing hostility between the Hema and the Ngiti, the greed of the traders and soldiers willing to profit at the expense of the local people, the prejudice, fear, mistrust and hatred between many people. More generally one would point to the pervasive culture of violence (itself arising from the context, as well as the meanings and beliefs arising in turn from that) in which it has become normal to solve disputes by force rather than by discussion.

It is in this domain of so-called *cultural violence* where the 'isms' of class, age, race and gender are to be found. It is here too that the deepening of hatred and stereotyping can lead to demonisation of the other and ultimately to dehumanisation. From here, ethnic cleansing, the elimination of the other, becomes acceptable, even necessary for wellbeing.

In British society examples of both structural and cultural forms of violence are not hard to find, though thankfully much less deadly than the examples above. While formal rules to benefit one group rather than another are mostly not permissible, in employment there is widespread, though illegal, racial and sexual discrimination. In matters of health, similarly invisible structures ensure that longevity and health are both substantially better in the south than the north of Britain. In schools, high drop out rates and poor exam results are disproportionately prevalent amongst Afro-Caribbean boys. Where these barriers come together they can create whole groups who find themselves excluded from mainstream life. Some of our urban council estates are the reservoirs for social exclusion.

Mental structures are just as prevalent and often act in support of these structural factors: asylum seekers are vilified in the media on the general and unproven assumption that they are here under false pretences and likely to be 'sponging' off the state. This has arguably led to changes in the way people perceive asylum seekers, and then to structural changes as the law has been changed to reduce the access of asylum seekers to Britain; and then to reduce the access of those here to benefits. Racial stereotyping is still common in many areas, though there is some evidence that the introduction of the Race Relations Act in 1976, with its many subsequent amendments, has led to changed attitudes as people have been compelled to change their behaviour. Sexism is still widespread in parts of society, and people who are over fifty often complain that there is a presumption in favour of younger people when trying to get a job.

One can extend this idea of cultural violence further to look at its main constituent dimensions, including, for example, the religious or spiritual domain. With this set of lenses one can, for instance, see the idea of a Chosen People as a prime case of cultural violence. Stemming as it does from a belief in a God 'out there' and a strong tradition of dualism (eg. good/evil, right/wrong) the question naturally arises: who is closest to God? Who gets chosen? Then the door is open to a division of people into chosen and not chosen, higher and lower, good and bad. Of course, by good fortune, the 'we' who promote this perspective happen to be the good, the chosen ones ourselves (Galtung, 1990).

Each act of violence can be seen in this overall framework: an interaction of cultural, structural and behavioural factors. Often the interaction is more like a chain reaction, a cycle of violence in which, for example attitudes (of anger) lead to violent behaviour (killing)

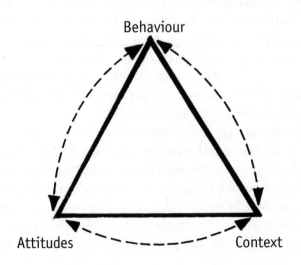

which itself changes the structure and context (another unavenged killing to add to the total) which in turn increases levels of fear which ... the cycle goes on until action is taken or exhaustion intrudes.

This diagram, often known as the ABC triangle, is adapted from Johan Galtung's original work and shows these concepts of behaviour, structure and attitude in close relationship.

In this, as with many situations of conflict, we have to note the influence of *vested interests*: there are many who benefit from restriction or damage to others, whether it is through the loss of opportunity or loss of liberty and life. At one level, depending on our values and the specific context, we might include in this category arms and drugs manufacturers and traders; at another we might point to men, especially white middle class men; at another to ourselves, whoever we are.

Examples abound. For instance, news reports in the British press have periodically highlighted Albanian criminal gangs who are engaged in trafficking women and children to the UK for the sex trade. The press reports, often highly indignant in tone, usually fail completely to note that the trade would not exist were there not a matching demand from British men, who are willing to pay to have sex with these women and children and therefore have a vested interest in the continuation of the trade.

So what?

Such a whole-hearted, inclusive analysis of violence will inevitably cause us to ask uncomfortable questions and it will have implications for how we might address the situation. Often peaceworkers have tended to ignore the vested interests, if only because they are often more difficult to gain access to, but they can be crucial to any long term resolution of injustice.

The ABC triangle can help to identify the dynamics of the violence we see about us, and plan more effective interventions. In the Congo situation, any intervention which did not take this underlying context into account might make a major error. For example, we might suggest a strengthening of the Ugandan military contingent, in order to maintain order. Having done our analysis we would know

that this would actually increase the violence as the Ugandan soldiers have a vested interest in violent conflict so that they can
continue their illegal trading activities in local minerals uninter-
rupted. Or we might suggest mediation. With the benefit of analysis,
and looking especially at the context, we would realise that the militias are too fragmented to be able to take part in mediation. Mediation
would probably be simply impracticable, or give undeserved credibility
to certain leaders, which could result in worse rivalries than already
exist.

Using this form of analysis can also point up why we sometimes
fail. In 1994, I was invited, with a fellow staff member of RTC, to
assist a group of Congolese colleagues near Bunia in training for leaders and advisers of the Hema and Ngiti. It was before the outbreak of
civil war and the training which we undertook, with a Congolese
Quaker from Kinshasa, focused on 'la résolution pacifique des conflits'
(peaceful resolution of conflicts). By maintaining the ambivalence that
the training might, or might not, be about the actual conflict they
were experiencing, the leaders were enabled both to attend (they could
not politically be seen to be participating in negotiations) and, in the
hours outside the main sessions, to reach a remarkable reconciliation.
Amidst much singing, the two chiefs ate and drank together for the
first time in several years. The facilitators had done their analysis well
as to the context and were open to, and happily surprised at, the outcome.

The final sessions of the workshop turned into a space for setting
up mechanisms for the maintenance of this fragile peace, including
regular communication between the chiefs, to be facilitated through
a motorbike in the absence of phones or postal service.

However, in the euphoria there was one element which no-one had
factored in. While the motorbike was available, the fuel for it was
becoming scarce, and very soon could not be obtained locally. The
peace broke down several months later, and it is not disingenuous to
say that it was partly due to the promise, and then the absence, of a
functioning motorbike. The resultant lack of communication and the
nonfulfilment of plans made at the workshop led to suspicions about
the good faith of those involved, which fed on the tensions inevitably

still present after many months of hostilities. Given the many hundreds of killings that have taken place since in the area, the human cost of this unexpected fuel shortage may, in retrospect, be judged to have been exceedingly high.

Analysing can also be intervening

Activists, such as those we met earlier, use this ABC triangle to analyse violence in many situations, from the very local to the global, to explore the dynamics, and to identify entry points: areas where it might be possible to do something to begin reversing the cycle of violence, and to find allies working on the same issue, perhaps at a different point on the triangle. It has been used by women to look at the kinds of violence they experience and plan action to address it.

Following this kind of process can also show up where the barriers are, and become an intervention in itself. I was using a version of this triangle with La Campagne des Apôtres de la Paix, a high ranking group of Burundians: politicians, soldiers, businesspeople, judges and civil servants from both Hutu and Tutsi communities. It was during a period of intermittent violence and the session took place just after a massacre in which some 200 Tutsis had been killed in the north of the country, following on a similar event not long before when the same had happened to the Hutus. We had begun a session by identifying the recent killings as a tragic example of violent behaviour in a very violent civil war. As we turned to look at the underlying context and culture of the situation, several of the Tutsis present declared: 'These people are insane. There is no reason, no structure to explain this. They must be killed.'

They had travelled so far down the road to dehumanising the opponent, despite having Hutus as friends, and members of the same group. Even the speaker of the parliament, a Tutsi member of the group, could not bring the discussion to order in the face of the violent feelings uncovered. The tension was such that it completely overwhelmed me. At the end of the session I lay prostrate in a side office for half an hour, overcome by the violence of the feelings expressed.

However, the group used this incident, and the evident impact on me, to reflect on what had happened and on relationships in the group. Their subsequent behaviour demonstrated that a real change had taken place. They have survived many other crises and are a continuing force, often at great personal risk to themselves, for dialogue in Burundi. If they had not confronted deep internal divisions such as this, I doubt if they would still be able to work together in the polarised atmosphere of Burundi.

In another instance the use of this triangle for analysis opened the way for Mohammed, a Palestinian, to announce to a Working with Conflict course group: 'Jews have no culture.' Subsequent discussions led to deeper reflection, and a progression from open rage to a position which allowed him to differentiate between individual Israelis. It also opened up a discussion on the way in which protagonists in conflict often get caught up in 'mirroring' each other's behaviour and attitudes: each side tends to exhibit the same behaviour, and have similar thoughts and emotions (for example, we are right, they are wrong; we are sincere, they are liars). This poses a major difficulty for those attempting to build trust between parties, as each act, however honestly undertaken, is open to misinterpretation: the worst motives tend to be ascribed to any action (for example, by offering talks they are really trying to exploit our weakness, give themselves time to rearm, undermine our resolve, and so on).

What, then, of peace?

There have therefore been considerable advances in the way we understand violence. But what can we say about peace? It seems to have a lack of clarity and edge: where is it? How do we know if we have it or not? Like health, it is easier to know when we do not have it, than when we do.

As a starting point we can agree with many exponents, Gandhi and Sydney Bailey among them, that peace is a process rather than an outcome. Peacebuilding is a lifelong, continuous task, relevant to all societies, all neighbourhoods. We never can achieve it wholly, and without fear of reversal. Peacebuilding is in many cases synonymous with social change, and peacebuilders are agents of change by another name, or catalysts.

A second pillar of our understanding is that peace is fundamentally concerned with relationships: relationships between individuals, organisations, communities, societies. Relationships are peaceful if they are equitable, reciprocal and promote the full growth and potential of each party involved. Peace work, or conflict transformation work, consists in analysing relationships which are critical in any situation, then promoting change as necessary through nonviolent means.

This kind of thinking can, however, be very discouraging to those in overtly violent situations who are striving for an end to killing. Are we saying that there is no end to that? The problem is that at least two meanings of the word 'peace' are being used.

Peace: cold and warm

The insights of peace studies can help again. If we define peace as, essentially, the absence of violence (in its three main dimensions as above of behaviour, attitude and context) we find we have a much clearer focus. By reducing or eliminating elements of violence in key relationships we bring into them elements of peace. If we help to reduce prejudice and build empathy and understanding between groups which are hostile to each other, we are building peace (changing attitudes). If we lobby for more resources to be made available for youth groups in an area of deprivation, that is peace work also (changing context). If we find ourselves in the midst of a confrontation and try to prevent any violence, that is peace work too (changing behaviour). All these elements, and more, are probably needed to make an observable difference in a given situation.

So if we work on violent behaviour, and succeed in eliminating it, do we have peace? Well, not complete peace, but we do have a crucial element of it: this kind of peace is often described as negative, weak, shallow or cold. It is essential if stability is to be established and livelihoods assured, but it is not in itself enough. In Northern Ireland feuding between loyalist paramilitaries has to be ended if the peace process is to resume, but its absence could not be described as peace. In Afghanistan during the rule of the Taliban there was a virtual end to random killing, a great improvement on the previous situation. However, human rights were often denied: women were not allowed to work and there were many other restrictions on people's freedom.

This was not peace in its fullness, as we strive for it. Quaker international mediation work has often been undertaken to reestablish a negative peace, on which other elements necessary for real peace can be built.

It is fundamental, therefore, to address the deeper structure of a violent conflict: the *culture* of fear, hatred and intolerance and the *context*, with its areas of exclusion, polarisation and the inevitable imbalances in power and access to resources. Without this work, the negative peace will weaken. With it we are gradually building warm, deep or positive peace.

Behaviour
Killing, Beating, Intimidation, Torture

VISIBLE VIOLENCE

Violence reduction to
promote 'negative peace'

LESS VISIBLE
VIOLENCE
under the surface

Work to change attitudes
and context as well as
violence reduction to
promote 'positive peace'

Sources of violence:
attitudes, feelings, values
*Hatred; Fear & mistrust;
Racism & sexism; Intolerance*

Structural or Institutional Violence
context, systems, structures
*Discrimination (eg in education, employ-
ment, healthcare); Global poverty; Denial
of rights & liberties; Segregation (eg apartheid); Manipulated histories*

Violence Triangle – Behaviour, Context, Attitude ©RTC

However, it may not always be possible to achieve genuinely peaceful relationships. In my neighbourhood in Birmingham, a small number of people living on the streets were harassing others and sometimes behaving aggressively, fuelled by alcohol. The local community organisation worked on all these three dimensions. They began action on several fronts: they researched the context, to find out why so many homeless people were in our area and what overnight facilities were available. They found that all the benefit offices in Birmingham had now stopped paying out over the counter except in our area. As a result our neighbourhood had become a magnet for those who had no bank account.

At the same time several people in the community organisation began to talk with the people concerned, explaining, with varying responses, the problem and the overnight facilities available, and suggesting they might like to spend the night in decent shelters. The council were requested to instruct other benefit offices to pay over the counter. When the problem persisted, the council were then lobbied first to change the bye-laws so that drinking alcohol on the street became an offence and later to take action through the police to remove the sleepers because of the public disturbance that was being caused.

From vicious to virtuous circles

If we see peace in this broader, strategic light it frees us from thinking we can, or need to, do it on our own – as if we could. We can work on a piece of it, and trust that others will work on another piece. If we are more strategic, we can go beyond hope and actively look for these others, build relationships with them, and even coordinate activities so that they reinforce each other. The happy fact is that, in the same way that we can observe a vicious circle, we can create virtuous circles also. Each time an action removes a pillar in the structure of violence the impact will affect the other dimensions too. And we can begin right where we are.

If people begin to dislike each other a little less, and even begin to have some acceptance of each other, they are less likely to believe malicious rumours about each other or to take action on the strength of these. If the context is thus stabilised there is the possibility of further, more far reaching work in a variety of ways.

Fear of peace

But one needs to remember: it is far easier, and quicker, to destroy change of this kind than to bring it about. And repairs take a long time. In many of the situations we face there are vested interests who have no wish for change to take place. In Jordan not long ago I was with an organisation closely involved in peace work in the region. From their many competing priorities for time and money they had decided to prioritise a seminar entitled 'The Fear of Peace'. It was going to look at all those who would stand to lose from a settlement between Israel and Palestine, and search for ways to reduce at least their perception of their losses. They were concerned that those who could lose from a settlement were powerful enough to make it fail altogether.

We need to be ready for things not to go as planned, at any level at which we are involved, and be determined.

SIGNPOSTS ▶

We have explored briefly some ideas about peace and violence, and found that under a magnifying glass they are more complicated than we might have thought. At the same time, these complexities offer us new possibilities to understand what is going on around us, and to think about effective ways of acting. We shall crystallise these a little later in the book, but we first need to look at our third key idea: conflict.

Far from being something to shun, as we may instinctively find ourselves doing, I want to suggest next that conflict is an essential ingredient of warm, deep peace. We cannot have one without the other. And that has major implications for peace work.

5

Peace needs conflict

Violence and nonviolence

Violence, we have seen, can be viewed as the opposite, the antithesis, of peace. It is ultimately the 'enemy'. Violent relationships destroy, limit potential, divide. And the effect, as we have also seen, reaches deep into the psyche. Speaking from the depths of his own experience, and that of the majority of South Africans, Steve Biko said in 1971: 'The most potent weapon in the hands of the oppressor is the mind of the oppressed' (Biko, ed. Stubbs 1996).

And yet, we also recognise that violence is sometimes used as a means to an end by natural allies of Quakers, people working for justice and freedom who believe change can only be brought about in this way. The first Intifada in Israel-Palestine was nonviolent. The second, beginning in September 2000, was based on the assumption that nonviolence had failed and that shootings and suicide bombings were the only effective weapons left to Palestinians. After several years it is not clear to anyone that violence was the better option. Nelson Mandela decided to fight the apartheid regime in South Africa with violence, having concluded, with colleagues, that it would not respond to nonviolence alone. However, in contrast to the second Intifada, where civilians have become the targets of suicide bombings, the targets of the African National Congress (ANC) armed wing, Umkhonto we Sizwe, were intended to be exclusively military and government installations – a tactical but also humanitarian decision.

Quakers can acknowledge their fundamental and practical support for the aspirations of the Palestinians, and others suffering repression, while differing on the means. Did nonviolence really fail? Has violence honestly paid off? There is often an unshakeable assumption amongst politicians and public alike that violence 'works' – the myth of redemptive violence, as Walter Wink describes it (Wink, 1998). Nonviolence, on the other hand, tends to be tested over a relatively brief period of time and can be rather quickly found wanting for lack of immediate results.

The invasion of Iraq potentially raises this question. If the outcome within say eighteen months to two years of the invasion is a more stable country, rebuilding its infrastructure and moving towards some form of accountable government (a very large 'if' at the time of writing, bearing in mind also the growing instability in Afghanistan, the previous object of 'regime change'), could we say that violence has 'worked'?

From a purely moral and spiritual stance our answer has I think to be no. There is no weighing in the balance of lives deliberately destroyed, each the bearers of the essence of God within them. Their loss is unacceptable, unequivocally. We utterly deny that it can be ethical to kill and maim, whether in the name of justice or domination. This can never be done in our name, in the name of members of the Religious Society of Friends who used to call themselves Friends of Truth.

What, though, of the pragmatic argument? How do we deal with the question 'is the world better as a result?' My own sense is that we need to have a short and a longer term perspective. In the short term it is possible to imagine that life will be better for the oppressed people of Iraq. After all they are freed from a brutal tyrant, and their lives may be beginning to resume with a measure of freedom. What about the longer term? This is where it is hard to be able to make a positive judgement. First, the likelihood of such an imposed regime surviving once the occupying powers have gone is remote. But more serious is the wider fallout: the emerging dominance of Israel in the region, backed by the USA, signals a shift in the power balance; the many future (ten years and more?) potential martyrs created by such a demonstration of invasive force; the weakening of the United Nations; the demonstration to the world at large that might continues to be right (whatever the rhetoric), which will undoubtedly be a lesson well learned by both present and future tyrants.

However, in looking thus at the negative effects, we should also be conscious that there have been positives too: for example, in Birmingham, where I live, opposition to the invasion brought Muslims, Christians, Hindus, black and white together to demonstrate for the first time in their thousands (a common enemy often has unifying effects) and has led to longer term contacts and exchange; the global movement against the war has created an unprecedented network which is capable of mobilising large numbers in case of future need; and the demonstration of unilateral military power has served to reinvigorate those arguing that there must be a better way.

If we need to talk the language of realpolitik these can be useful points of argument. However, the active nonviolent witness is that violence in all its forms is to be resisted by peaceful means. And members are prepared to carry the price of that commitment. In the dichotomy between pragmatists and believers in nonviolence, most Quakers stand as believers, willing to carry it through as love in action, because it is right, even if nonviolence does not seem to deliver the hoped-for results.

Local as well as global relevance

In thus coming to a clearer sense of what we mean by violence and peace, and what our commitment is, we have seen how these concepts apply with equal force to international, national and local situations. And in Chapter 2 we looked at how these different levels are inextricably linked, one to the other. There is therefore no intellectually honest way in which we can stand in the light and then, with integrity, take steps to try to influence the violence we perceive in Iraq, Zimbabwe or North Korea, for example, and ignore the progressive alienation and 'criminal' behaviour of significant groups on our doorstep.

And yet the local situation often seems a lot more difficult to disentangle and address. Is it an illusion that one can see more clearly what needs to happen several thousand miles away than very close to home? In part I think it is. As outsiders we can never fully pierce the deep crust of shared history, culture and understandings, let alone language, which make up the fabric of any social situation. There is a kind of illusory clarity which can dissipate as we get to learn more about the complexities. On the other hand being outsiders does give one a freedom from the bonds and blindfolds which are so hard to see, let alone remove, when one is part and parcel of a situation, especially one where tension and conflict are endemic.

Another reason perhaps why many of us prefer to work on the distant issue rather than the local seems to me to be our fear of conflict. For all our beliefs that peace work and witness should be at the heart of the Society, when we are faced with conflict close at hand, in our meetings for example, there is a powerful urge to smooth things over, or to avoid the contentious issues altogether.

What do we mean by conflict?

If we are to explore this question, it will help if we look more closely at what we mean by conflict. In everyday life the words 'conflict' and 'violence' are often taken to mean the same thing. The two are used almost interchangeably in the media, especially with regard to international issues. In conflict transformation and peace work, by contrast, the concept of conflict has been reclaimed. It has of itself no causal or other link with violence. Rather the reverse: conflict is simply what happens in relationships when people have goals which are, or seem to be, divergent or incompatible.

With this set of lenses, we can see that conflict is inevitable: people are born male or female, with different backgrounds, religions, values, experiences, aspirations. There are differences in access to power, resources and education, and technology is always challenging the way we do things and the way people are employed, or unemployed. It is inconceivable that any society and organisation should not experience conflict as a matter of course. It is however highly conceivable, and often the case, that people try to ignore or suppress conflict.

Conflict as a threat to order

In more traditional societies, conflict is often seen as a dangerous threat to the social order. Disagreement is therefore quickly covered over by referring to precedent, or by invoking the elders as arbitrators, often buttressed by proverbial sayings. Some societies do not have a word which translates directly as 'conflict', and are oriented towards avoiding or suppressing it. I vividly remember being asked to run a two week seminar for teachers in Fiji, when RTC was just starting. The subject, ostensibly, was disorder in the schools. There did not seem to be a great deal of school-level disorder, however, and I was a little bemused. Finally on the penultimate day, my persistent questioning was met with a very delayed response: the organisers of the seminar were actually going to use the methods I was sharing with them to address the deep splits and conflicts at national level in the management of the education system between Indians and Fijians which, in their view, threatened the very continuation of the system. They had simply not wanted to say this to me, or openly acknowledge that there was a problem.

Industrialised societies also experience the suppression of conflict. By opening up a situation to question, conflict threatens the status quo and introduces the possibility of change. Elites who have got more than their share of the cake, however defined, tend to be creative in finding ways to avoid or eliminate serious conflict which involves them. They do however often seek to foment conflict amongst those they rule, on the 'divide and rule' principle, or allow it to develop unchallenged. We might cite media reporting in the UK of bomb plots intertwined with confused government policy on asylum and immigration.

Intensifying conflict for just outcomes

People working for change, however, in community development or human rights for example, are often seeking not to resolve or reduce conflict, but to intensify it: that is, to make it more clearly visible and thus to raise the level of urgency to deal with it in the community affected, and beyond. To do this, depending on their analysis of the conflict, they will sometimes use approaches which address the imbalance of power in a situation, often trying to empower the weaker group to exercise more influence and, if possible, simultaneously attempting to weaken the grip of the powerholders.

Community workers in South Africa were doing just this during the mid to late twentieth century, backed by international agencies. They had to do it rather secretly for fear of being unmasked as political meddlers, exposing their partners to attack in South Africa itself, and losing support at home. In Oxfam, during the 1980s, the ANC were known in team discussions as the 'doctors', and the South West Africa People's Organisation (SWAPO) in Namibia went by the name of the 'nurses'. Since no one bothered to tell me of this code, I was more than a little mystified when I initially joined the staff at the apparent size of the health programme in the region.

Similar conflict-creative approaches are used in South America and other areas where there are substantial marginalised populations. However they need to be very carefully carried out. In heavily repressive states there is a high price to be paid for resistance, and it is local activists, not the international agencies, who are likely to take the pain.

In the UK this proactive approach seems to be less common than it used to be, as social work has become focused on the difficulties of individual families rather than the wider context. Previously – in the 1960s and 1970s – some social workers would, for example, have seen it as part of their job to facilitate people living on disadvantaged housing estates to come together, discuss critical issues and lobby for change, perhaps at the level of the local council.

Conflict resolution approaches

Most conflicts are solved or managed without violence or a high cost of any kind. If not, our societies would have fallen apart long ago. However, the huge loss of life which armed conflict gives rise to has undoubtedly been a major spur in developing new approaches to its resolution. Equally the widespread occurrence of domestic violence in many countries has been a driving force behind innovative approaches in family therapy as well as community-level provision of services. At neighbourhood level, mediation schemes have multiplied to deal with disputes and given birth to systematic training and accreditation schemes. Much thought has therefore gone worldwide into developing coherent approaches to conflict resolution, from a variety of disciplines and perspectives. There is inevitably a huge variation between them.

A major difference is that between conflict resolution and conflict transformation. Conflict resolution tends to be focused on a specific conflict, and seeks to address both the behaviour and causes of it. Conflict transformation is broader: it addresses the wider situation as well, including latent or hidden tensions which may in future erupt into visible conflicts, and their causes. It is therefore inevitably concerned with social and political change (see Chapter 3, Lives that Speak, for a more elaborate definition of conflict transformation).

Most approaches, however, and certainly that of conflict transformation, tend to prioritise the development of skills in dealing with conflict behaviour such as mediation and negotiation, as well as communication and interpersonal skills. They include a focus on three basic areas:

- ❂ *analysis*: including the different types of conflict, underlying factors and dynamics, the main parties and issues
- ❂ *working with conflict*: examining behaviour within conflict and attempting to influence it, and developing plans to reach and sustain a resolution
- ❂ *reconciliation*: finding ways to heal the rifts and address the grievances and hurts which inevitably emerge when there is conflict. If these are not dealt with fully, however constructive the outcome, the conflict will probably reemerge·

Analysis of conflict
Types of conflict
The diagram on the next page sets out a very basic typology which can help one to think about types of conflict and stimulate ideas about what should be done, if anything, in any situation. It suggests that there are two main variables in conflicts: behaviour and goals. Each of these can in any conflict be clashing (incompatible) or not. Sometimes it is the behaviour which is clashing, sometimes it is the goals. Sometimes everything is in harmony. By juxtaposing the two axes in the diagram we can envisage four different kinds of situation: harmony, surface conflict, latent conflict and open conflict. All of these situations can be found at any level of a society or organisation, or in our own families and meetings.

An example may clarify. In your organisation things seem to be going well: you and your colleagues are in the harmony box. However, some important new information (the office will close tomorrow at 2pm), heard in haste by one of the administrative staff, is incorrectly relayed to others (the office will close today at 2pm), who act on it

Analysing conflict: the square

Conflict occurs when two or more parties have, or think they have, incompatible goals, and adopt attitudes and behaviours which reflect this.

In order to understand more deeply what conflict is, it can help to focus on two elements in this definition: behaviour (which is basic to any relationship) and goals (what you want to achieve). The model below identifies different kinds of conflict according to these two elements.

Compatibility of Goals and Behaviour

	GOALS	
	COMPATIBLE GOALS	INCOMPATIBLE GOALS
COMPATIBLE BEHAVIOUR	HARMONY	LATENT CONFLICT
INCOMPATIBLE BEHAVIOUR	SURFACE CONFLICT	OPEN CONFLICT

© RTC, 1996

and upset others, before becoming offended themselves at the response to their mistake. This incident could be isolated. However, it might also be seen as a symptom of a deeper malaise: a neglect by senior staff of the needs of administrative staff, for example, or vice versa. If this is so, the issue may be recognised and dealt with, and changes made in the way the organisation functions. However, it may also be ignored, perhaps because there is no opportunity to deal with it or because not enough people wish to do so. Perhaps even because those who decide the agenda of staff meetings do not wish matters such as this to be discussed.

If such matters are not dealt with in a reasonable time, and the resentment level is high, there is every chance that the conflict will burst into the open. This is likely to be unpredictable, perhaps coming at a moment when nerves are frayed and minds and bodies tired. Then there is open anger, and hurtful words and accusations are flung about, often without forethought, with the force of an erupting volcano.

There is then a period of time during which a reconciliation can take place. This usually requires, in private, some acknowledgement by one or both parties of their part in the conflict, apologies as appropriate and, in public, an attempt to find a way to prevent this happening again: perhaps by introducing a new procedure, or by one or more people changing their behaviour in some way.

One can then return in due course to the harmony box. Only for the process to begin again, in some other part of the organisation, probably over quite different issues. Not only is this process unavoidable in a healthy organisation. It is absolutely necessary for it to remain dynamic and energetic. There is a mass of published literature concerning the importance and positive impact of conflict in commercial and other organisations.

Conflict is thus endemic in a healthy social organism at all levels, from family and friends to community, national and international. It is notable in this diagram that none of the boxes is labelled 'peace', even the one on the top left. Harmony can be maintained for a while, but, if prolonged, it can become stifling and lead to stagnation. A peaceful, lively organism needs all these dimensions of conflict, and to have mechanisms to analyse, mediate and integrate them.

Different forms of intervention are needed for different kinds of conflict, or stages of a particular conflict. A surface conflict often needs essentially improved information and communication. A latent conflict will probably need an approach which addresses the underlying factors or dynamics, while open conflict will very likely need initially some action to cool emotions and move the attention from a focus on the people or parties to the issues at the heart of the conflict.

Multiple truths

In dealing with everyday events such as the example above, we rapidly perceive another cornerstone of peace work: that there is no objective truth. Views will differ as to what is important, memories about specific events will vary, different values will suggest different issues and dilemmas as priorities.

This is of course a feature of all work in the social sphere, but it seems often especially hard for those involved in conflicts to acknowledge that they do not have access to the objective reality, however hard they work at it. They can set out the *factual* truth: i.e. what physically happened, and when. Even this is still possibly arguable, but only because the evidence (what were the precise details, or consequences?) is not to hand. However, the *narrative* or *moral* truth (the way events and trends are linked up to create meaning and history) is filtered through our values, our experience and information sources, and constructed accordingly.

In Britain the different communities in our cities see many situations from their different vantage points, some prioritising religion and culture, while others emphasise equality and gender. For example, the hijab – the headscarf worn by Muslim women – is now much more widely worn, than, say, twenty years ago. From the wearers' perspective, the fundamental motivation behind this development may be a reassertion of religious and cultural identity, and of sexual privacy, in the face of the perceived threat from the majority community. Amongst the majority community the development seems to be perceived in several contrasting ways: a growing sense of challenge to the dominance of their values (women should be seen), an invitation perhaps to look more closely at the wearer, or as a reminder of the perceived gender inequality in Islam. It is easy to see how such differing narratives can lead to tensions, as well as creative discussion.

This also happens frequently on the wider scale. In a dialogue workshop I was facilitating between Palestinians and Israelis a moment came when an Israeli headmaster began telling the group about the work he and his (Israeli) school were doing on behalf of the Palestinians. They were creating opportunities in the school for pupils to talk about their attitudes to Palestinians and the Intifada, something most Israeli schools would not do for political reasons or for fear of trouble from the parents. In addition they were collecting food and clothing and taking these to give to Palestinians in a West Bank city nearby who were suffering severely from the lengthy curfews and lack of availability of basic materials. 'We are doing all we can,' he said. 'And, what we need is partners. Why won't you Palestinians accept our goodwill and work with us?'

There was a long pause before a Palestinian woman replied: 'Thank you for your charity. But keep it. We don't want it. We don't even want to be here talking with you. Our people at home see us as collaborating. We do not want to be your partners. We don't have time or energy for it. If you want to help us, work on your own government and society. There is no room for anything else now.'

The Israeli had taken personal risks with his own community in order to offer help; the recipient saw only a patronising gesture in return for the risks she was taking with her community.

Acceptance of multiple truths is key

In these situations, close to home as well as distant, the essential task is not to try to establish agreement on one 'objective' view of the situation, but to find ways to enable each side to acknowledge that the other side has its own equally sincerely held narrative. If they are able to acknowledge this they may be willing to listen to each other. And if they are willing to listen, they may begin to accept that their own narrative may have questions about it too, which need addressing.

Can they then move to accept a way forward which values diversity, rather than uniformity, and is inclusive of each other's stories? Quaker mediators have traditionally used this approach. As yet it is honoured more in the breach by those operating through more formal channels. Would a British government feel able, for example, to listen carefully and consult with those involved in gang warfare in Britain's streets rather than pronounce its own view and rush to judgement for public consumption?

I wonder how many Quaker meetings see themselves as having a role to play in local issues such as this, especially in promoting opportunities for facilitated dialogue and for the different sides to hear each other's stories and grievances. In Lambeth, after the 1981 Brixton uprising and the subsequent Scarman Inquiry, Quakers took the initiative with others to set up the Lambeth Police Community Consultative Group. This provides a space for the different communities to meet and raise issues with each other so that they can be addressed well before the consequences erupt on the streets. There is a growing and urgent need for this work, as events, the media, and government policy conbine to marginalise Muslims in Britain.

Awareness of our personal ways of handling conflict is an important foundation for action

In deciding whether, and how, to act, we can usefully ask ourselves at the outset: How do I deal with conflict myself? How could I anticipate and deal better with conflicts?

In answering these questions it can be very helpful to reflect on the styles which we habitually use to deal with conflict. The diagram opposite sets out a range of possible options in any situation.

This framework is based on the assumption that our behaviour in conflict is governed by two goals which are in tension: the wish to get our own way, and the wish to maintain relationships or at least avoid making enemies. If we get our own way, but do it at the expense of isolation or outright opposition from others, we may be losing too much, except perhaps in extreme circumstances where conscience, or a particular concern, dictates. If on the other hand we prioritise relationships with others above our goals, we may never achieve what we wish and end up frustrated.

There are, then, five main styles: avoiding, controlling, accommodating, compromising and problem-solving. It is important to note that

STYLES OF CONFLICT MANAGEMENT

CONTROLLING

"Do it my way"

Strategies:
control, compete, force, coerce, fight

Impatient with dialogue and information gathering

Prefers others to:
avoid or accommodate

High Concern for Personal Goals

PROBLEM-SOLVING

"Let's try to resolve this together"

Strategies:
information gathering, dialogue, looking for alternatives, seeking 'win-win' solution

Prefers others to:
problem-solve or compromise

COMPROMISING

"I'll give a little if you do the same"

Strategies:
reduce expectations, bargain, give & take, 'split the difference'

Cautious but open

Prefers others to:
compromise or accommodate

Low Concern for Relationships

High Concern for Relationships

AVOIDING

"Conflict? What conflict?"

Strategies:
flee, avoid, deny, ignore, withdraw, delay

Refuses dialogue, gathers no information

Prefers others to:
avoid

Low Concern for Personal Goals

ACCOMMODATING

"Whatever you say would be fine with me"

Strategies:
agree, appease, smooth over differences, ignore disagreements, give in

Interested in other's information and approval

Prefers others to:
control

this framework points to the wide range of options available to us. It does not indicate that there is one ideal response. Each may be the right one in a particular circumstance, depending on culture and context. For example, you may feel that controlling is an unworthy style, as it involves compelling someone to accept a solution to the problem. However, if your child is about to cross the street and is refusing to listen to your reasoned arguments why she should wait until the cars have gone, controlling is probably the best way to save your child's life.

A general point which can emerge from this kind of thinking is that most of us could look more often at the possibilities for problem-solving, where the aim is to achieve one's goal at the same time as strengthening relationships with others involved. Compromise, where we each lose and gain something, is often what we settle for, but it is inherently unstable as both parties have not got what they really want, and they have also lost something. For problem-solving to work at least three factors need to be in place: safe space to work through the problem without disturbance, a rough equality of power in the situation, and a willingness on all sides to solve the problem.

Looking at ourselves

It can be instructive to use this framework to look more closely at the dynamics of conflict at national and international level. It is also useful to help us look at our own ways of dealing with conflict, at work and at home, and perhaps also those used predominantly in our meetings. It can help us question whether we are making full use of the possibilities. Most people, and most organisations in my experience, tend to have a default setting when conflict occurs. They avoid, or control, or compromise as a matter of course. This has the advantage of predictability, and therefore routine, but scores low on creativity and imagination, qualities which are crucial in building and maintaining fruitful relationships – and peace.

Interests, identity and ethnicity

Some conflicts are essentially over *interests*: these can often be dealt with by examining more deeply what people are really trying to gain, and enabling them to find common ground. Many of the more intractable conflicts however are primarily about *identity*. Who are 'we', who are 'they', why are 'they' threatening us? In situations where there is a clash of identities, a resolution is hard to come by: from inner city Birmingham, where white, Asian and Afro-Caribbean gangs confront each other in prolonged low intensity ritual, to Northern Ireland, to the Balkans and the Middle East, the intractabilities are similar.

Identity becomes an issue usually only when there is insecurity and thus fear. When the state, or law enforcement, is weak, and there are historical grievances which may not have been fully addressed, people may be looking for protection. There is then a space for leaders to mobilise 'their' people and promise them safety around a particular form of belonging: perhaps a fundamentalist form of their religion, or the assertion of an ethnic identity which has been largely forgotten in the previous relative peace.

The basic insights of conflict transformation suggest that we need to create ways of organising ourselves at all levels: state, organisation, neighbourhood and family, in each of which people can belong freely to the groups they choose, and express that belonging in ways which are not perceived as a threat to others. At these times people can live to the full with the multiple identities which are a natural feature of peaceful societies, as they perform different roles in their lives.

Reconciliation

Conflicts require reconciliation

Any conflict which is at all deep is laden with emotion, and often involves feelings of grievance and guilt. It would be facile to suggest that once a conflict is over the parties to it can continue as usual, as if nothing had happened. And, if they do, it often means that there are rocks just beneath the surface of the future relationship. In my experience some rebuilding of relationships is nearly always needed.

What needs to happen for reconciliation to occur? The following elements are likely to be part of any creative outcome:

❂ *Truth* – acknowledging the facts about what happened as fully and undefensively as possible, and listening attentively to the other's truth

⊗ *Justice* – accepting responsibility for one's actions and being
   willing to repair any damage and restore the relationship
⊗ *Forgiveness* – being willing to overcome one's anger and to
   forgive the other once acknowledgement has been made, and
   to heal any hurts.

Although there is no space here to explore the idea of forgiveness
fully, it cannot go without mention. The capacity to forgive, to live in
a perpetual state of forgiving others, was urged by Jesus so often in
his ministry, up to his very death. It has a spiritual imperative about
it. But what about the practicalities in a world of many religions and
cultural traditions?

Often, and most fundamentally, my experience has been that we
need to forgive ourselves for the mistakes we have made, and will continue to make, before we can forgive others. In forgiving ourselves we
free ourselves from remorse and self-hatred.

This enables us to forgive others also for what they have done.
When we forgive others they in turn can be freed from the burden of
what they have done.

We, by so doing, are also freed from the shackles of bitterness and
the desire for vengeance for what has been done to us. Both these have
the capacity to imprison us and deprive us of our future. Forgiveness is
in this sense a key to liberation and the transformation of relationships.

But we have to be careful not to make our idea of forgiveness rather
trite and over-simplified. Sometimes there is no 'other' to forgive: they
are anonymous, untraceable. Or the act is simply too destructive,
and the pain too excruciating, for us to be able to forgive. Sometimes
the perpetrator refuses to acknowledge in any way what they have
done – or at least that we have difficulty with what we perceive them
to have done. In these cases we are left with our anger, which needs
to be acknowledged and then channelled creatively. We have then to
take care to direct our anger outwards, when the instinctive response
may be to harbour it, where it may accumulate mental energy and
feed the inner crocodile of revenge. In some situations the most that
can be achieved is acceptance, which gives the capacity to let go and
move on.

Breaking the cycle of revenge

In Kenya the change of government in 2003 led to the departure from government of a number of close associates of the former president who had used their office corruptly for their own personal gain. They had become very unpopular as a result, and made many enemies. One such man returned to his estates far away from the capital, and very soon there was an attack on his land and both property and crops were destroyed. He could no longer use government resources to impose his will. He was essentially powerless. Peacenet, a local organisation active in peace work in the region, heard of the attack and got in touch with him directly. They expressed sorrow at what had happened and sent one of their 'rapid response' teams to assess the damage with him and to see if they could find out who had done it. They told him they could not condone what he had done in government, but nevertheless he should be treated fairly, and they were opposed to any attempt at revenge.

The agency remained actively concerned with the issue. While the police did not find the perpetrators, agency staff raised questions about it with the local community and the elders, asking them to look at what was happening. They raised such questions as: Was violence and revenge actually the way to get what they wanted? What would be a better way?

Over time, as the man realised that this was a genuine approach, he began to respond: he had expected to be treated with the disdain with which he had treated others, but he had in fact been treated with forbearance, even by some of those affected by his corrupt actions. He has since quietly begun to look for ways to make amends. The potential for forgiveness had triggered a change – how radical is not yet clear. It would have been so easy for Peacenet to shrug their shoulders and say: 'He deserved it', which would have given the cycle of violence another twist.

Reconciliation is a stage, not peace itself

But none of this adds up yet to peace as we have seen it earlier. Truth, justice and forgiveness are crucial constituents of reconciliation. For peace – positive peace – to emerge, there needs also to be some agreement about how to go forward, some analysis about how to address the underlying structure and attitudes, and a procedure for how things will be done differently to avoid future problems of the same nature.

Frequently, in my experience, reconciliation is confused with peace. They are in fact quite distinct. Negative peace – the absence of hurtful or violent behaviour – is essential as a prerequisite for reconciliation. Once that has happened, we all know from our own experience how repairs need to be done if the relationship is to be restored. There needs, if at all possible, to be a 'making-up'.

At national level, truth and reconciliation commissions try to carry out this process for whole populations. They are, though, almost always focused on expressing the perceived truth of what took place. This is important in itself as a beginning of healing; however, reparation and justice are crucial to a different future, and much more difficult to implement. Some of the perpetrators of violence are nearly always well placed in the new order, and may hold an effective veto over its future. There is therefore often a trade-off between the need for an end to killing, on the one hand, and justice on the other. And in a divided society, one person's justice can be, or seem to be, another's revenge. Impunity is often the outcome, at least for a while. 'We will not punish you for what you have done provided you do not do it any more.'

Reconciliation and culture

This 'smoothing' approach is consistent with many customary methods of reconciliation in Africa. The Mato Oput ceremony amongst the Acholis in Uganda, for example, involves rituals in which perpetrators of violence acknowledge their misdeeds, express sorrow, are purified and accepted back into their communities. This ceremony has been used widely in attempts to reintegrate children abducted and turned into killers by the Lords Resistance Army. It certainly seems effective as a psychological mechanism, enabling children to have the courage to come out of the bush and to begin to face their past, and the community to forgive them.

But it has a cost, in that, since there is effectively no reparation or punishment required, others may draw the lesson that they can commit crimes and then go through the ceremony without having to be punished. It may therefore put at risk the positive, sustained peace in the future for which people are yearning.

Peace is forgotten, until we lose it

Reconciliation, as we have seen, consists essentially in the rebuilding of relationships. For positive, warm peace my experience is that we need to translate strong relationships into durable systems and procedures and rethink our institutions. This is the stage so often ignored. Once the conflict is over, and relationships apparently restored or at least stable, attention moves on. Perhaps a report is written which lists the causes and solutions. But the hidden grievances which have not been heard, let alone addressed, the inequalities and exclusions which may have been behind the earlier difficulties will surface again, probably more damagingly, unless structures are created to deal with them.

The violence in Britain's northern cities during the late 1990s and early 2000s caused a great deal of public angst at the time. Bradford, Burnley, Blackburn, Oldham were etched briefly on people's minds. Much government money was allocated to dealing with the causes and making practical improvements for the future. The question was, what changes and how to implement them? However, the timescale of remedial action was often so short (government budgets operate only a year at a time for the most part), and commitment by those involved consequently restricted, that outcomes must have been much less than the potential.

RTC was working with UK government agencies on new programmes for training and supporting community-level facilitators in conflict resolution in the most volatile city areas of the UK. At the start of the programmes the participants did not know if they would be able to continue, even into a second year. Motivation and commitment were low: in one series of three trainings the participants insisted on changing the venue twice, thus more than doubling the accommodation cost. Not infrequently individuals would take whole days out, despite avowing the relevance and practicality of the work being done.

This programme looked good on paper, and perhaps in a manifesto. But it ran the risk of being largely window-dressing despite the best efforts of those organising it, when what was needed was committed

follow-through to build change into the areas where the riots had happened, and those where nothing had as yet happened. The cost of
this may (one certainly hopes not) become evident in the future when
inter-community relationships fragment again, and violence breaks
out once more. Serious, in contrast to token, peacebuilding is long
term and often low profile.

SIGNPOSTS

In this book so far we have seen some of the insights coming from the
field of conflict transformation. We have seen that conflict and violence are very different from each other. Violence is the antithesis of
peace. Conflict, on the other hand, is indispensable, an inevitable part
of our lives and our society and essential for social and political change.
As we work for peace we need not to run away from conflict, but to
make it serve us and the Quaker inspiration which fills us. This runs
counter to the cultural norms of many of us. Can we take up the challenge and embrace conflict, even – especially – in our own meetings?

There are other sources where deeper knowledge of themes we
have touched on in this chapter is available. My purpose here is more
simply to share some of the learning from peace work in progress
around the world, to learn from this and focus our minds on the crucial importance of conflict in the process of change. We are moving
towards the question: so what does this mean for us, as members of
the Religious Society of Friends, seeking to live out our commitment
to peace and justice?

In the next chapters we build on earlier sections in this book, and
seek to face up to the dire state of the planet, and of ourselves as part
of humankind on it. If we do not take risks now, we shall only have
to take greater risks later. Can we build on our expanded idea of the
components of warm or deep peace, incorporating of course the ecological dimension, and begin to challenge and transform violence in
behaviour, structures and attitudes wherever we encounter it? There
is no need to travel. Ourselves and our homes are the scene of struggle as much as the world at large. We will try to clarify how we can be
both personal and political in our search for peace and justice.

6

Waging peace: contradicting, conspiring, confronting

Our challenge
'One generation all that is left to save world, report warns.' The headlines stare at me from the paper lying open in front as I write this. The article, concerning the 20th report of the Worldwatch Institute, goes on to list the ways in which humanity is impacting on the precious biosphere which supports life on the planet. It occasionally refers to a sign of hope, things that can be done, but the phrase 'there is a lack of political will' stares at me repeatedly from the page. Why do we lack the will to act on the problems that threaten us? How do we reconnect with these life threatening issues before it is too late?

A considerable number of Quakers individually strive to live in harmony with creation, recognising their global connections. However, many of us, while absorbing the media reports and scientific evidence, continue to act as though the context will remain the same. Maybe we have seen too many of these reports to take them seriously any more. Maybe we simply do not know how to take them into account. We can feel secure as long as we do not look out of our circle too far.

Quakers have a powerful history of struggle on many social issues, including peace and justice. We have had to change strategy and tactics as times changed, but the core remains the same: recognising that of God within every one of us and allowing that of God to shine out and work in the world.

What is the challenge now? We can learn much from those we met earlier in this book. And we need to go on to do our own analysis, as they have done in their situations, knowing that the world is so interconnected that the impact of what we do, however small, will travel well beyond our shores. Doing a small thing is not doing nothing. It is doing something.

A stark picture

First, we can usefully clarify our frame of reference. We are talking about a challenge that combines two Quaker testimonies: to peace, and to equality. At one end of the spectrum peace work continues to be about ending 'deadly quarrels', a task as vital now as it has ever been. Our message, and our experience, is that violent means beget violent outcomes, in the short or longer term. At the other end of the spectrum peace work merges into work for the good society: we are talking about equal rights for all, happiness, physical and mental health, wellbeing. The task is to work for a world in which those states of mind and body become a reality for people everywhere. We do this first because it is our deepest impulse, the expression of our true nature, of God. We do it also because we know that unless we work at these deeper levels of mind, culture and structure, we do not address the causes of war, injustice and oppression: cold peace easily turns into cold – then hot – war.

Knowing this, we observe ourselves as actors in a world characterised by unpredictable and persistent violent behaviour, from the home to the globe, underpinned by a culture and structure of violence and domination.

Three competing dogmas

We could see ourselves as caught between three sets of dogma, three fundamentalisms. One is Muslim, that of the Wahhabite Sunnis, from Saudi Arabia, who are behind Al Qaida. One is the Christian, born again variety predominant in the USA, to which George Bush belongs. Both have a clear view on who is right and who is wrong, who is evil and who is good. They are mirror images of each other, and both of them represent desperately inadequate ways of viewing the world. The third set of dogma is market capitalism, which stretches its tentacles everywhere in the name of freedom and democracy.

Conventional politics, at the moment when we need it most, has almost everywhere become sterile. However 'democratic' the country, political leaders rarely acknowledge the depth of the global challenge, and even more rarely take steps to address the critical issues. Environmental issues are well down the to-do list. Violence, or the threat of violence – and specifically terrorism – is met by secret and overt force, and by attacks on countries thought to be harbouring terrorists, or harbouring other assets the powerful might want, such as oil. The causes of terrorism, state or individual, are not seriously addressed: our government does not willingly look at underlying structures, perhaps for fear of admitting that serious, and costly, changes in attitudes and policy are needed. As we have seen, there is little or no willingness to be self-critical, to question the contribution of the USA and its allies to the events of 9/11.

Thus the global disparities and injustices are not addressed. The same old messages are beaten out on the drums: we are right (might is right). The poor and excluded of every country are honoured in the rhetoric, but lose out. In growing numbers those that can flee their countries, becoming economic migrants, refugees or asylum seekers.

Honesty and Realism

To write these words, and no doubt to read them, can feel disempowering, and depressing. And yet they need to be faced if we are to be honest with ourselves, and to live our lives authentically. We can only walk cheerfully over the world, as George Fox asks us, if we have seen and acknowledged the abyss in front of us (Fox 1656; *Quaker faith & practice* 1995 §19.32).

A further piece of honesty is also required: this time about humankind. Research in the human sciences over recent years has strongly challenged the idea that humans are basically peaceful if only they are not incited to violence. The !Kung San of the Kalahari, for example, who used to be cited when I was at school as archetypal examples of how, given natural conditions, humans will live harmoniously with each other, have been shown to have homicide rates higher than those in many US cities, and hold dismissive, contemptuous attitudes not only towards non-San people but also to those amongst the San who are not relatives. Similar characteristics have been identified amongst other peoples once thought to be naturally nonviolent (Konner, 2002).

However, there is also strong evidence that cultural contexts influence the level of violence: anthropologists tell us, for example, that societies where husband-wife intimacy is high and tasks are shared are among the least violent. On the other hand in those where males are frequently segregated from women and children, and male-male inter-action is high, the levels of violence are high.

Furthermore, looking for a moment at our evolutionary past, it is perhaps reassuring that studies of behaviour amongst monkeys and apes suggest that reconciliation is a fundamental aspect of behaviour of primates. If humans, in common with all primates, have a predis-position to aggression in certain situations, they also have a similar inclination to forgiveness which has evolved over some thirty million years. Reconciliation, from this ethological perspective, is an inbuilt need and owes nothing to religion or moral codes. We are in this sense working with the grain (de Waal, 1989).

There is a little further reassurance from the social sciences: during an experiment in which people's brains were monitored while they played a game called the Prisoner's Dilemma, researchers found that, when people made cooperative moves, their brains showed the stan-dard signs of pleasurable activity. This did not occur when they made competing moves. The pleasurable response happened before they knew the outcome of the game, or whether the other player had coop-erated. Humans, it would seem, experience and act on social feelings towards others, even if these are not reciprocated. And this gives them a positive feeling about themselves: virtue is in this way its own reward (Layard, 2003).

In summary, social scientists are telling us that we need to be real-istic about what can be achieved. There are inbuilt propensities both to violence and to reconciliation. Violence can be reduced, even become dormant for periods, but not eradicated. Reconciliation and reciprocity are part of our nature, but we do not yet know enough about what conditions assist these impulses. Recognising these reali-ties may open the way more clearly to effective methods of violence prevention.

Realism also requires us to look at what violence is doing to human-ity and its civilisation. We can be amazed at the cost of organised violence, and of the forces needed to sustain it, globally and locally, and we can be still more amazed at the myth, assiduously maintained, that violence works as a way of solving problems. There is a widespread, and highly arguable, presumption that nonviolence is a luxury which has to be dispensed with when conflicts get difficult. The public are fed, until most believe it, assumptions that war, or the threat of war, is necessary to bring peace. 'The myth of redemptive violence is the simplest, laziest, most exciting, uncomplicated irrational and primitive depiction of evil the world has ever known' (Wink, 1998). It is not surprising that some of the people in our cities and schools have learned this lesson so well and that a culture of violence is found on our streets.

What then to do?

What are the implications of all this for us? The essential message of unconditional love does not change. The task, as all the sages tell us, is to transform ourselves, and our relationships, from the inside out. To be the future we want to see, now. To live the kingdom.

I live in hope that the Society of Friends, as individuals and institutionally, will recover the prophetic vision and proclaim it through our lives. We need to do this for ourselves as individuals, for our families and friends, for the wider world of which we are a part. And fundamentally because the spirit within us, the Inner Light, allows us to do nothing else.

How then, do we translate this into practice?

Becoming signs of contradiction

Begin at the beginning. Whatever our lifestyle, it is almost inevitable that we are complicit, if not active participants, in the global system of dominance outlined earlier, in which the majority of the world is left without the basic requirements of a decent life and the remainder is fed daily with the great lie: 'The more you have the happier you are.'

The least requirement of us, as individuals and as members of the Religious Society of Friends, Friends of Truth, is surely that we strive to reduce our compliance in what has unquestionably become a deadly system: to ourselves, to our fellow human beings and to the planet.

Much of what we may be called to do is to highlight the contradictions in our secular society, local, national and global, to dissent from them, to contradict them: i.e. to speak out against, and to let our lives speak. We may need to invest more than our spare time, and to reconsider how we prepare and present what we are saying and doing. If we are to make our voices heard in the sophisticated world of twenty-first century communications we must educate and challenge ourselves to the best of our abilities, and seek out every possible ally. Further, we can be signs, public signposts to a different way of being and acting. And this is bound to come with a cost: to our pockets, almost certainly, but perhaps also to our reputations and respectability.

Some examples of contradiction

Trident Ploughshares is a group of people dedicated to campaigning against nuclear weapons, and specifically the UK nuclear Trident submarine fleet. They are pointing up the contradiction between the UK's commitment to international law and its possession of weapons of mass destruction. Made up of ordinary people from all walks of life and of all ages, they use all nonviolent means to bring the issue to public attention. Most of their actions end up in court, and they are often acquitted, on evidence that nuclear weapons are illegal. Over four years the 190 members from all over the country have totalled 1,790 arrests, 380 trials and 1,680 days in jail. This is not for everyone, but these are not rent-a-mob in any way: the choices they have made began in lives built on careers and families. Their willingness to go to court, and to prison if necessary, ensures that a crucial issue receives constant publicity.

In a more localised example, in 1981, during the war over the Falklands/Malvinas, a group of people in Bristol, including a number of Quakers, decided they had to do something to speak out against the war and the tide of nationalism that went with it. Voices on their own were not being heard. They did their research and found that much of the Argentinian army was made up of conscripts who were paid very little. If they were killed their families received nothing at all in compensation. So the ad hoc group (who called themselves with some irony SAG: Special Action Group) decided to launch a public fund to support families of conscripts who were killed by the British Army. While the amount raised was always going to be small, the point would, the group calculated, not be lost on the British media or public: 'This war should not be being fought. We have a responsibility to those who are casualties of it.' The British Army were volunteers, and families could receive widows' pensions if necessary, so they were at least looked after financially.

The fund was launched simply by issuing a few press releases to the national and local press. The response was rapid. *The Times* and the *Daily Telegraph* ran matter-of-fact articles, with details of where to send contributions. Radio 4 gave an interview on 'The World Tonight'. Local television gave interviews. The tabloid press put it on the front or nearby pages with lurid headlines and depicted SAG generally as a group of thinly disguised Argentinian sympathisers. They phoned for interviews, often trying to trap members into quotes which would betray the group as 'quislings' or supporters of dictatorship. Anything but look at the issue of the rights and wrongs of the war, which the group continued to try to raise.

Local papers, interestingly, took a more human interest angle (Who were these people? Why could they possibly want to do this?), and in Bristol there was hot debate, with both support and some sporadic hostility.

The fund raised a total of some £1,700, with contributions from all over the country, often with verbal wishes of support attached. However there was a sting in the tail. After the war was over none of the main UK banks would handle the transfer of the proceeds to the human rights organisation in Argentina with whom arrangements had been made by SAG. Finally it was, with difficulty, handled by the International Red Cross, and reports were later received that the fund did provide assistance for several families.

Looking at its overall effect, the action was well timed for maximum impact. It succeeded in raising – albeit briefly – the issues surrounding the war amongst the public in Britain and provided some space for alternative views to be aired. As a small sign of contradiction it pointed to the many negative and unpublicised effects of war and challenged people to think about their own response.

Less positively, the action was never documented or tied into other peace-related work which groups were doing. The learning from it which could have been channelled into future actions was never done, as individuals took up their busy lives again. It was in that sense a rather typically amateur approach to peace work – an immediate, time-bound reaction to a perceived affront – contrasted with Trident Ploughshares, whose more professional approach aims to be more strategic and long term. The issue of amateurism and professionalism in peace work is raised again towards the end of Chapter 8.

Local as well as global

Signs of contradiction can happen at all levels, the very local as well as the national and international, and they do not have to involve der-ring-do or high levels of activity.

❂ When Joy, a Quaker in Birmingham, decided to give up her job as a well paid university lecturer in order to devote herself to contemplation and the inner life, she herself became a sign of contradiction. She challenged others' assumptions about what constitutes worthwhile work, about busyness, and about the value of prayer and contemplation. In starting a meditation group for local people she created – and now sustains – opportunities for others to make this journey too, most with much less of a costly commitment than she has made. And she thereby supports others who are taking a more physically active role for change.

❂ A group of others in the neighbourhood are operating a LETS scheme, whereby people barter and exchange their skills, rather than put a financial value on them. In so doing they meet their own needs more effectively and cheaply and send out a signal about the need to put human values first, rather than setting a financial value on each skill. LETS schemes are operating in many parts of Britain now.

❂ In Porto Alegre, Brazil, the city's governing Workers Party decided fifteen years ago to draw up the budget through an elaborate and extensive process of public participation, not by fiat, as previous administrations had done – and most cities in the world do. The result, according to observers,

has been a redistribution of wealth, a reduction of poverty
and the virtual elimination of corruption. It has become a
working experiment in participatory democracy. The Workers
Party now rules the country through the election of President
da Silva.

Each of these examples is in fact 'peace work': they seek in different ways to address both the behaviour and the underlying structure
of the global to local system of domination and profit which allows
lives to be lost, more often, in reality, for lack of resources than as a
result of war and open violence. They are also creating new alternatives: signs of contradiction which point onwards to new ways of
living and working as well as attracting attention to the issues and
injustices of the present. And, crucially, they are not isolated acts but
strategically undertaken to build a wider constituency for change.

There are no prescriptions or instruction manuals for this work.
Wherever we are, the question is posed: do we wish to stand out
against the negative effects of the global system, and build alternatives
or are we active cogs in it? If we are in both camps (which many of us
almost inevitably are), are we happy with the balance we have struck?

The Commitments

A friend recently gave me a copy of the 'Ten Commitments', an adap-
tation of the Ten Commandments written by a US Rabbi, Michael
Lerner (Lerner [undated]). They seem to me to be a creative way of
framing what I have termed here 'contradiction'. I quote three of them
below:

6. Do not murder

Aware of the suffering caused by wars, environmental irresponsi-
bility, and eruptions of violence, I vow to recognize the sanctity of
life and not to passively participate in social practices that are
destructive of the lives of others. I will resist the perpetrators of violence and oppression of others, the poisoners of our environment
and those who demean others or encourage acts of violence. Aware
that much violence is the irrational and often self-destructive

response to the absence of love and caring, I vow to show more loving and caring energy to everyone around me, to take the time to know others more deeply, and to struggle for a world which provides everyone with recognition and spiritual nourishment.

8. Do not steal

Aware of the suffering caused by an unjust distribution of the world's resources, exploitation and theft, I vow to practice generosity, to share what I have, and to not keep anything that should belong to others while working for a wise use of the goods and services that are available. I will not hoard what I have, and especially will not hoard love. I will support a fairer redistribution of the wealth of the planet so that everyone has adequate material wellbeing, recognizing that contemporary global inequalities in wealth are often the resultant of colonialism, genocide, slavery, theft and the imposition of monetary and trade policies by the powerful on the powerless. In the meantime, I will do my best to support the homeless and others who are in need.

10. Do not covet

Aware of the suffering caused by excessive consumption of the world's resources, I vow to rejoice in what I have and to live a life of ethical consumption governed by a recognition that the world's resources are already strained and by a desire to promote ecological sustainability and material modesty. I vow to see the success of others as an inspiration rather than as detracting from my own sufficiency and to cultivate in myself and others the sense that I have enough and that I am enough, and that there is enough for everyone.

From contradiction to conspiracy

Working for change is often lonely. Most of us need to find ways of linking with others, for support, advice and accompaniment – and to help avoid pitfalls such as pride and being quick to judge those who do not share our perspective ('Lord, I thank you that I am better than other people are').

Quaker meetings may provide one means of this support: indeed

Benchmarks

Inspired as we may be by taking a stand in this way, one of the
difficulties may be self delusion. Are we doing what think we are?
I may think I am standing out against, for example, covert race or
sex discrimination in my workplace, but is this how I am seen?

Whatever level or issue is under consideration, you might usefully
ask yourself some questions such as these, perhaps in a meeting for
clearness, which Quakers sometimes hold to enable a member to test
a concern. They may help to raise awareness of difficult personal
issues, and to promote reflective discussion:

Fear: Am I ever afraid because of this?

Conflict: Do people get annoyed or in conflict with me over this?

Ridicule: Do people ever laugh at me over this?

Giving up: Do I ever assess progress and wonder if I am wasting
my time?

Cost: Do I ever wonder if I can sustain the cost in time or money
over this?

Suffering: Have I ever suffered or lost out because of this?

Gain: Am I gaining practical insights and experience from this?

Support: Do I receive support from people specifically because of
this? Do I reciprocate?

Self-awareness: Does this lead me to question my own motivation,
even occasionally my sanity?

the hope is that increasingly this will be so as members of the Society
become more concerned at the divergence between rhetoric and reality in our secular society. Of course there are many other circles and
networks in which we move made up of people whose values are similar to our own.

In a healthy democracy there would be space for dialogue and coalition-building for change on these issues within the representative system. With the fossilisation of the political system in the UK, we need to build our own flexible structures of support and challenge. One might call these structures *conspiracies*, but not hidden conspiracies. These are open and inclusive groupings, aimed at social and political contradiction and transformation, designed to challenge at root the various forms of oppression and injustice we observe in ourselves, our surroundings and in the wider world. Conspiracies which are based on the core values of human needs and human security worldwide.

A conspiracy (literally, from the Latin, to breathe together) means in this sense much more than a network, or a pressure group, though it may take both forms. Its members have a wider vision, a deeper, strategic commitment, a stronger resistance to obstacles and failure.

At present, many of us belong to groups which are focused around a particular issue, such as asylum seekers, community relations, a specific war or international debt. They become conspiracies when they start to explore and articulate the wider framework in which their specific issue arises, and look for political expression. This is necessary in any case because we are dealing with diverse symptoms of a system out of balance. Solving any one will only push the pressure in another direction: for example, if we achieve a more sensitive policy towards asylum seekers it may exacerbate conflicts at community level. If we stop new road building, congestion will worsen unless car dependence is tackled.

Examples of conspiracies

Sometimes signs of contradiction grow into conspiracies. In the case of Porto Alegre, mentioned above, the working experiment in democracy by the city led to it hosting, in 2000, the first annual World Social Forum, the nearest thing, some say, to a people's United Nations. Held annually at the same time as the business-led World Economic Forum in Davos, Switzerland, over 100,000 activists for peace and justice from all over the world now come for four days to share experience and discuss participatory democracy, social economics and alternatives to war. Peace is a basic motivation in the forum: one activist in 2002 was quoted as saying: 'If we are to end war, we need a new kind of globalisation, based on democracy and social justice.'

The Coalition for Peace in Africa (COPA) started life as a group of African peace and development workers who wanted to find ways to work together and promote 'African solutions to African problems'. After initially functioning in an entirely voluntary manner COPA received substantial funding, and hired a coordinator and regional workers to help widen the network and develop its activities. It began to acquire a reputation for conducting highly successful courses for practitioners from across the continent, and providing advice and assistance to development and relief agencies working in areas of conflict.

Then, disaster. The coordinator, a South African Catholic priest, was found to be embezzling large amounts of COPA's income. The small COPA office had to close, and the staff were laid off. All funds were exhausted. This might have been the end of the story, but the members were determined not to let COPA die. It was then that the deeper commitments came out: they were appalled at what this would do to the image of Africans and African organisations. They were outraged at the way corruption had found its way into their organisation committed to social and political change.

As a result, they began legal proceedings against the coordinator and rebuilt COPA. They were determined to keep the name, although it would have been easier to change it and begin again. They found ways to 'piggy back' their meetings on the back of other work. Two hard years later they had reformed themselves and re-established a voluntary coordinator. A year further on they were running new courses, taking on new pieces of work and had voluntary regional coordinators in place.

COPA is hugely stronger for having refused to lie down. It has turned an abject failure into a great strength. In addition to restarting its basic work it has trumpeted its living contradiction of corruption and challenged the wider image of Africans. It is a fine example of an open conspiracy.

From conspiracy to confrontation

If contradiction is to go beyond personal fulfilment and satisfaction it surely needs to lead beyond conspiracies to confrontation, with the issues, with the people who embody them and with the wider system. COPA chose to confront the corrupt priest, rather than connive in silence. Earlier in this book we saw how true peacebuilding needs conflict at its heart: surface, latent and open conflict are necessary companions of harmony. Without them harmony becomes oppressive and stagnant. We need to find ways of confronting which are nonviolent and make use of all the sources of power at our disposal. In this it can be helpful to have in mind also the matrix of conflict styles: we have many options in the way we address differences and we can help each other become more skilled in the use of these.

The Citizens Organising Foundation (COF) works to change the nature of life in areas of deprivation and social exclusion in the UK. Inspired by the work of Saul Alinsky in the USA it strives to enable ordinary, often poor people to analyse and articulate their needs and to organise themselves to achieve them. They build coalitions across faith groups (Muslims, Christians and Sikhs are all involved), trade unions and local associations. They use the techniques of active nonviolence, adapted and elaborated to suit urban communities, to take effective action and build more socially just and engaged communities.

Backed by substantial Quaker money, and with a Quaker as the main initiator since its inception in 1989, COF is serious about results and about the long term. Its campaigns are focused on the needs that local people identify through an extensive period of listening and inquiry. The results are announced publicly by the local group and those with responsibility challenged to redress the grievance.

The main focus in the London area is the Living Wage for London campaign (defined as £6.50 per hour in 2003). When they do not comply, employers are confronted, whether government, health authority or private company, by TELCO, The East London Citizens Organisation. In one case concerning an international company, TELCO formed its own local association for the cleaners, the lowest paid staff of the company, as the trade unions in the area were not interested. Largely as a result, the cleaners achieved substantially better wages quite quickly, but TELCO's interest is in all the company's workers, many of whom are overseas, so the campaign continued.

The cleaners continued to provide intelligence to TELCO of the company's intentions, having access through their job to noticeboards and documents left casually on desks, and being well placed to overhear informal conversations.

Tactics in this campaign have included buying shares in the company in order to raise the wage issue at the AGM ('always use methods out of the experience of the opponent' is one of the key methods of COF), and cultivating the local free newspaper so that the issue is often on the front page. COF created public prizes for a newspaper and journalist each year, and have awarded them with publicity and acclaim. They have also managed to cultivate the support of a good number of high level contacts to add credibility to the organisation, including nationally prominent people in the media, banking, religion and politics.

Waging global peace

There are many cases now where individuals, acting together, have changed the way things happen not only at local or regional level, but at global level.

An impressive recent example, if still unsuccessful in the short term, arose as a result of the invasion of Iraq. Desperate as this event was in many ways it has had some positive outcomes, notably in the way it served to raise the awareness of people all over the world about war and the way the world is. Perhaps most encouraging was the birth of a genuinely global anti-war movement. This has combined contradiction, conspiracy and confrontation in a quite revolutionary way, using modern communications technology to share information and ideas across the world – as well as across our sometimes fractured local communities – and to mobilise people for vigils, demonstrations and direct action. It is a movement which is waging peace in every nonviolent way it knows, and will in future invent. As a result a huge global conversation has been taking place about the very legitimacy of war, about the costs, about alternatives to violent methods of conflict resolution. It has vast potential, both as a support for peace-promoting work and as an obstacle to governments wishing to mobilise their people for war in the future.

Dr Robert Muller, a former UN assistant general secretary, who was present at the founding of the UN and has worked in it all his life, gave voice to this hopeful view shortly before the invasion took place:

> Never before in the history of the world has there
> been a global, visible, public, viable, open dialogue and
> conversation about the very legitimacy of war. This is
> a miracle. It is happening now – every day, every hour –
> waging peace through a global conversation. (Twist,
> 2003)

Conversation

And that ultimately is what we are trying to do through contradicting, conspiring and confronting. We are trying to have a public conversation about peace and justice beyond the PLUs (People Like Us), with those who really are like us but may have forgotten; with those, whether or not in political power, who either will not accept the legitimacy of views which differ from theirs, or patronise them as being unrealistic. We are seeking to create the space in which we can be listened to as well as listen, to discuss and differ, and to assert the opportunities we see for a better world, and the dangers that lurk.

Is this all too political?

We may feel that much of the above is too political for us: especially if we are members of the *Religious* Society of Friends. It may help to remind ourselves here that we have been looking in much of this chapter at what happens when people come together.

Each person's part is small, in accordance with what they feel able and called to do. The question is less, then, what we can do, than: can we stir ourselves?

It may help also to remind ourselves that Jesus himself practised all these things:

❂ he pointed up the contradictions in the values of his own people in many ways: for example, by his embodiment and espousal of unconditional love towards enemies as well as friends, by his inclusion of Gentiles as well as Jews in the call to repentance and salvation, by his treating women in ways that were radical for his time and place

❂ he conspired openly and effectively by recruiting and training a small group of followers, and then appealing to the wider population to adopt his values

❂ he confronted the authorities, both Jewish and Roman, religious and secular, with a radically different way of living and behaving, while setting himself against any form of violence.

George Fox, in his turn, was also an exponent of these strategies. It was the contradictions that he saw in the priests and churches of his day, and their inability to recognise the inward light in each and every person which moved him to 'bring people off from…men's inventions and windy doctrines', to 'declare against them all' and to 'cry for justice' (Fox, ed. Nickalls 1952, 1997, p.36).

As people gathered around him, and began to organise, they were perceived as seditious and were persecuted: all meetings for worship of more than four people (except Anglican services) were made illegal, and the refusal to swear oaths, to take off their hats or to use the second person plural as a sign of deference, in themselves simply outward signs of the values of this expanding group, became points of persecution.

And Fox knew that to confront the authorities was a necessity if they were to listen. His vision, as it developed, was of a spiritual truth allied to a programme of social reform, essentially concerned with justice, sincerity and integrity. By proclaiming this at every opportunity, in words and actions, at whatever cost to himself and his followers, he and they were able to get their truth heard, across the country and up to Cromwell himself.

There have been many other exemplars down the years, known and unknown. We can be their heirs.

Here is a challenge laid down to us today, as every day, which we can take up, or walk away from.

SIGNPOSTS ❯

We have talked in this chapter of big ideas: of contradiction, conspiracy and confrontation. None of it is superhuman. All of it is being done, unproclaimed, in many places by people like us, people like those we met earlier in the book. They have analysed their situation and responded where they are, as they can.

All this could seem above our heads, for other people, brave people or those who are really up against it. How can it apply to me? Like the boiled frog, we cannot easily see or react to the slowly growing threat, and it is easier to assume that somehow things will get better. However, the water is getting warmer. And all that we have talked of falls well within our heritage as Quakers, and as Christians called to live unconditional love on earth.

As Quakers, a crucial part of our response is to know that we are acting 'in the light'.

We shall look in the next chapter at the word that has come to describe that state: concern. We shall look more closely at what acting 'under concern' entails, and consider the risks and opportunities this gives rise to.

7

Acting out of concern

Beauty ever ancient ever new
Too late have I loved you
I was outside and you were within me
And I never found you
Until I found you within myself.

St Augustine of Hippo, *Confessions* Book X Chapter 27 (adapted)

Making time to listen

At the core of many lives that speak of beauty, love and justice, is a profound and disciplined inner life. We are such busy people. We are doing so much to put the world to rights, or to earn a living, that we do not pause. Unless, that is, we are ill or exhausted. When we think about the needs of the world, and the culture of violence which surrounds us, we may want to reply: but we have no time to do more. Almost certainly we will not find time for prayer, except when we are at our wits' end.

And that, I believe, is crucial if we are to break the bonds which hold the 'system' in place within us. For our busyness is also, for many of us I suspect, an escape, from having to look closely at our lives and our relationships, at ourselves; from having to listen to our inner voice.

I have found it necessary, like many others, to leave behind old images of prayer, in which I was taught to talk to God and ask for what I needed. It seemed meaningless. For a number of years that meant that I did not pray, at least not in any conventional sense. But I found increasingly that I no longer had the inner resources to do the work for development and peace which I was engaged in. I was drying up or, to my horror, becoming like the people I was trying to oppose and change. I became prey to anger, and quick to judge other people, especially perhaps those who were on the same 'side' as me.

I also noticed this tendency in others, especially those working for peace. A peace education project, for example, in which the staff developed such antipathy to each other that they would no longer talk to each other, and communicated only through terse notes. They could still do the work in schools, for a time, but the heart was dead: they were at war with each other.

Meditation

On coming to Birmingham over ten years ago, I began to feel more strongly that attendance at meeting for worship and other functions organised by my local meeting were not meeting my needs. I was fortunate to discover in due course that a meditation group was starting in the neighbourhood. It was, and is, affiliated to the Christian Meditation Centre in London. I am not a good 'joiner', but to my surprise I have been a regular member of the group for some eight years now. We – usually no more than six to eight of us – meet to meditate for thirty minutes once a week, and try to maintain the individual, private discipline of two sessions of meditation per day, one in the morning and the other in the evening.

We use a word, or mantra, suggested by John Main, a former Dominican monk, who has traced the origins of this kind of prayer back to the fourth century desert fathers, who themselves got the tradition from their forebears. We have the barest minimum of 'rules' for how to meditate. (Repeat and listen to the mantra continuously from the beginning to the end of the session.) We discuss our practice, and issues arising for us, regularly in the group.

What is happening? It is hard to answer that question, partly because the whole practice is about leaving thoughts, feelings, hopes and fears behind: there is no thinking involved. It is premised on the fact that the real 'I' is not contained by thought, and cannot be conceived by thought or analysis. Furthermore, effect is not part of the calculus of doing it. One meditates because it is as basic as breathing, as some teachers say.

Certainly, at a psychological level, I find that the practice induces calm, and reduces the background noise of emotions and thoughts. I find myself less likely to get drawn into confrontations without proper reflection beforehand. The internal volcano is pacified.

Beyond that, meditation has become for me what others call prayer. It is a time when I am no longer the centre of my universe. The ego is temporarily put aside: that part of myself which asserts that it is myself, which sees itself as a separate being, struggling for independent existence in a world where one has to fight for power to maintain one's individuality and survive. Each session of meditation seems to weaken the ego's power-hungry aspects a fraction, allowing other aspects to emerge, so that, one hopes, one gradually becomes the self one has the potential to be. More space is created for Love, for God, for the Great Spirit.

Building awareness

It is important, I feel, to realise that this ego is partly made up of social conventions, outer beliefs we have internalised. It is not just an internal process of self-realisation which we are talking about here. These internalised beliefs come from our upbringing and become part of our makeup too. They can relate, for example, to our gender roles – where men and women can have very deep and different understandings about their own relative status. It can relate also to politics: my experience in Zaire in the 1980s was that many Christians seemed successfully to free themselves from some of the internal constraints of the ego, often as members of a charismatic sect, but could not manage to free themselves from being active participants in the corrupt, nepotistic political and economic system which dominated their working lives.

Walter Wink puts this approach to prayer much better than I can:

> Prayer is never a private act disconnected from day-to-day realities. It is, rather, the interior battlefield where the decisive victory is won before any engagement in the outer world is even possible. If we have not undergone that inner liberation in which the individual strands of the net in which we are caught are severed, one by one, our activism may merely reflect one or another counter-ideology . . . We may simply be caught up in a new collective passion, and fail to discover the possibilities

God is pressing for here and now. Unprotected by prayer,
our social activism runs the danger of becoming self-
justifying good works. As our inner resources atrophy,
the wells of love run dry and we are slowly changed into
the likeness of the beast. (Wink, 1989, p.181)

Becoming like the 'beast'

Whatever the method we choose, it seems that we ignore prayer at our
peril. Not just because our inner wells dry up, but because also we risk
becoming like the 'beast': like the 'enemies' we are fighting.

The mechanisms whereby this happens are complex, but we come
to see in the world 'out there' the negative forces in ourselves which
we cannot deal with. At the same time we draw into our inner selves
the negative forces which we see in the world. The outcome, if
unchecked, is that the hurts and wounds we carry with us from earlier times in our lives, and from childhood, feed on these influences.
Our 'shadows' are strengthened and our behaviour becomes increasingly contrary to what we think we are working and living for.

I knew the director of a conflict resolution organisation, itself committed to peace, equal rights and dialogue, who became so remote and
manipulative in his dealings with people that he acquired a far-reaching reputation for his dismissive and arrogant behaviour, something
which in his work he and his colleague were continually trying to
overcome. His remoteness also made it all but impossible for his colleagues to raise these issues with him, and he finally had to be
compulsorily, if gently, removed.

The same thing happens also to organisations working against
violence. They easily import into the heart of their operations the
worst aspects of the chaos they are struggling against outside:
despair, disconnectedness, and dismissal of other points of view.
They thus become traumatised, casualties of the situation instead
of healers of it.

At a more mundane level many of us will be familiar with someone, perhaps in a Quaker meeting, who is totally committed to one
cause, and is rather dismissive of those who do not see it this way
nor offer the same commitment.

In a nutshell, the struggle against injustice and violence can make us behave unjustly and violently ourselves. Unless, that is, we work consistently at our inner selves, build our own awareness and constantly challenge the preconceived ideas and assumptions we bring to each situation. Government ministers in Zimbabwe are today responsible for one of the most oppressive regimes in the the world. I worked on a farm with some of them during the liberation struggle of the nineteen seventies. They were idealistic and thoroughly committed to social justice. What has so publicly and dramatically happened to them can so easily, given appropriate circumstances, happen to us also. This is crucial inner work that needs to be done, and will take our time.

Enemies and anger

And, paradoxically, at this point we find we need our enemies or opponents: they are a real gift to us. Because when we look at those we feel hostile to, and examine our own thoughts and emotions towards them, we find there, in those aspects where we have the strongest feelings, elements of our own shadow. Jesus' injunction, 'First take the log out of your own eye, and then you will see clearly to take the speck out of your neighbour's eye,' was surely pointing at just this phenomenon. We have to address the issues in ourselves, because they can prevent us from seeing clearly the issues for others, but also because they help us to grow.

None of this should be taken to suggest that we need to eliminate our anger. Sometimes peace workers, even (especially?) Quakers, assume that if they show anger it is a fault: they have not worked enough on their inner conflicts and resentments. On the contrary, anger is in my experience a major source of energy to combat injustice, both for oneself and, through empathy, for others.

I am angry that 12.5 million people (22% of the population) in the UK are living below the poverty line (Rowntree 2003), while others have riches beyond their conceivable needs and deserts. The effects of poverty on physical and mental health are well documented. And I feel deeply frustrated that, while this is a subject which is frequently aired amongst political parties and in the media, very little is actually done to change it. I need to find a way to channel that anger and frustration into positive action, and beware of allowing it to become counterproductive.

A major way to do that is to focus on the problem: poverty and the severely unequal distribution of income and wealth in this case, and to separate this out, as far as humanly possible, from the particular individuals who manifest the problem most acutely. If we are to do this successfully we will of course need to develop our own awareness of the tensions we carry within us as a result of our life experience, and be wary of the tripwires which are likely to destabilise us unexpectedly.

Feedback and challenge

Feedback, as many know but few practise, is an important way of enabling each other to grow in awareness and competence, and to increase the effectiveness of any initiative for peace and related goals. In my experience it needs to be done carefully, at a moment when emotions are stable and there is enough time to talk things through. At moments of stress, comments meant well may be seen as attacks, and resisted. Feedback needs also to contain both areas of affirmation and aspects where there could be improvement.

It is easy to establish a process whereby people involved in a peace programme, for example, give each other positive feedback: what they appreciate about each other, how they valued what each other has done and so on. The difficulty with this is that it is dishonest. And this tends to show itself as the process becomes ever harder to sustain. It is not possible to believe in one's strengths without looking at the weaker aspects, any more than it is possible to have light without dark. I have seen organisations where affirmation is the order of every day, to the point where everyone believes that they are doing everything excellently. In these situations, where people are underperforming, they often do not pick up the message until too late, when some critical mistake is made. And then they are devastated.

So honest feedback and its sister, challenge, are central to our peacebuilding work. And perhaps to our Quaker witness and worship, if we dare.

Concern and power

As we reflect deeply on ourselves and our capacities in relation to the outside world, we are putting in the building blocks to support a life which speaks increasingly of truth, justice and peace. And we have found the right place for the Spirit, the architect, at the heart of the building process. In so doing, it is my experience that we also discover new conviction and power within ourselves.

So much has been said and written about power, that I hesitate to add to it here. The distinctions between coercive or 'hard' power (the ability to command and enforce) and persuasive or 'soft' power (the ability to bring about more or less willing cooperation through persuasion and inspiration) are probably familiar. They are important to our thinking about how those who take a nonviolent approach to social and political issues can bring about change.

The seemingly infinite variety of forms of 'soft' power help to explain the many different ways which we know from our experience that change happens. In a recent course at RTC, participants – from some twenty countries – came up with the list below when asked to name the kinds of soft power that they found important in their work.

education	networks	language	expertise
hope	faith	skill	empathy
knowledge	determination	finance	persuasion
love	belief	religion	identity
health	personality	inspiration	

We are, conclusively, more powerful than we think. We give our power away all the time, without thinking. When we act out of concern – out of deep conviction, shared, tested and confirmed with others – our power, or rather the power that works through us, can be remarkable, and quite unpredictable.

From my own experience, and reflecting on those whom I have worked with and observed in different parts of the world, the following seem to be crucial elements in taking a concern forward. We need to be: inspired, ready, risk-taking, inclusive, enabling, and strategic.

98 SPIRITED LIVING

Inspiration

'For thine is the kingdom, the power and the glory.' How often I used
to recite those words. Only recently have I begun to have a glimmer
of what they mean. If we are to respond from the heart, from God, our
deepest place, to the world's needs, and to our neighbour's, the inspiration will come to us. We will not, cannot, devise it, or possess it or
control it. This is maddening to those of us trying to live with modern
concepts of strategy and long term planning. For the spirit 'blows
where it wills'. To be possessed by a concern is to feel oneself in the
hands of an impulse that is ruthless, creative and hopeful, yet also
gentle, loving and profoundly fulfilling.

Readiness

The Spirit is everywhere trying to find a home where love and compassion and the struggle for justice can take root. Wherever there is
fertile ground the seeds come and germinate. Our task, if we are so
moved, is to be ready and able to receive the message, to be open to
what the Spirit is asking of us.

Risk

To be fully ready for, attuned to, the inspiration we have to take risks
– to be already taking risks: with our security, with our reputations,
with our career paths. We need to have developed a habit of living
adventurously. And that goes against much of what our conventional
selves, bolstered by advertising in all its forms, and fears fostered by
the media, may see as important.

Concern may well show us new actions that need to be taken,
quite new shapes and formations that need to be created, new relationships and vision. We may feel impelled to leave our secure jobs.
The question forces itself insistently on us, requiring an answer in
kind, not in theory: where is our security?

Inclusiveness

The power of the Spirit, of a concern, lodges itself within our deepest
selves and turns everything upside down. It takes us with it in direc-
tions we would not have chosen. But it is not confined to us. We are

presented with a plant, which for its survival needs to propagate and to mutate. The moment we try to capture it and enclose it in our own safe space it becomes sterile.

There are many examples of true inspiration which have flowered, then quickly withered, as those with whom the inspiration lodged try to make it their own. There is a line in a hymn which my children used to sing: 'Love is something if you give it away. You end up having more.'

The nature of true concern is that it *is* communion, and that requires openness to others and a willingness to share, or cede, ownership.

Enabling

As the concern makes its home in you, so it teaches you how small you, as an individual, are. It becomes clear that things are happening around and beyond you for which you are not responsible. The choice is faced: am I going to claim this initiative for myself (thus bolstering my insecure sense of who I am in the world), or am I going to accept the reality, that the responsibility lies deeper than I know, and beyond my control.

The first route is a shortcut to negating the action taken: one's own clarity becomes clouded and the ideas and hopes of others become excluded. The second means finding new sources of power within oneself, continued risk-taking, and glorious uncertainty.

It means seeking out and making space for others to develop their confidence and skills to the maximum.

Strategy

If in putting our concerns into practice, whether as individuals or in our organisations, we find ourselves deciding on an action, implementing it and then immediately planning another, we are probably not being effective. It is crucial to have a vision, to develop an analysis and then a strategy that will bring us towards that vision. Further, we need to ensure that we are learning from the steps we have already taken: at a personal level, through feedback and challenge for example, and at the level of the wider initiative or organisation. The strategy can then be adjusted in the light of this assessment.

Having said that, life, we know, does not follow predictable pathways. At RTC we joke that we have a 'rolling strategy', by which we mean we know what we ought to be doing, but we are flexible in the face of changing circumstances. The question remains: *how* flexible should we be?

These qualities have suggested themselves to me, often too late and with some inevitable pain, out of my experience in education, aid and peace work.

Some of them may seem rather prescriptive, at odds with the free workings of the spirit. My own belief is that they can serve us well in going beyond the well intentioned but slightly random activity for peace and justice of inspired individuals and groups to a professionalism in the best sense of the word, imbued with generosity of spirit. As individuals and Quaker organisations we might find it useful to look at factors such as these, alter them as necessary to correspond with our own understanding and experience, and then apply them to our own work.

In undertaking our analysis and strategy-building there is good advice available. There are a number of useful books, some of which are recommended at the end, which offer helpful suggestions, if needed, to supplement and improve what we already are doing.

Time-bankruptcy

It is clear that time is a major issue. We are many of us extremely busy, and cannot easily see our way to doing much, if any, more. None of what is written here should make anyone feel guilty, or desperate. It may indeed be a matter of making some life-changing decisions to create for ourselves more time and energy, as we reflect on the issues and our own capacities. We may decide to change, or leave, our paid work. We may take a critical look at our existing 'peacework' and see whether we are using the time and resources we have to greatest effect.

We may, on the other end of the scale, reorientate slightly what we are already doing to make space for some form of peace witness and action. It may be a question of looking again at our own lifestyles and standard of living, perhaps then freeing up resources on a regular basis so that others with more time can do this work.

I would suggest that in our own decisions we seek to continually push beyond and expand our 'comfort zone'. Have you considered tithing, either in time or money? This could be a tangible sign of our commitment, and a rather delightful mirror image of the imposed tithing of the seventeenth century, which Quakers refused and were imprisoned for.

Hope and resistance

During the nineteen-seventies, in pre-independence Zimbabwe, I visited an old man in a cold and remote mountainous area. He was living in a heavily concealed tiny shelter made of branches. His name was Chief Rekayi Tangwena. In the dark interior, sitting on the damp earth floor, this highly respected man explained that he was there to lead his tribe's struggle for their land which the Smith regime had expropriated. Their huts had already been burned down, and their crops destroyed, six times. Each time they built a hut, or planted crops, the police came to destroy them. Yet he and his people were utterly determined. They simply began again, supported, crucially, by a network of people from near and far, who brought essentials such as food and clothing and provided the media and human rights groups with continuous information about the struggle. A few years later, against all likelihood at the time 1 visited him, the Tangwena were able to resettle in their lands.

I have talked at the beginning of this book of setting our sails so that we can catch the wind, or rather, so the wind can catch us. To get that far we need that invisible dynamo: hope. We need to believe that things can and will be different.

I have worked with groups who have lost hope that things can change. They have not been able to imagine a future where their own struggles for peace have been at least partially successful and things have improved. Hopelessness acts as a glue, sticking them firmly to the ground. It is as if they have allowed despair to colonise their futures.

They at least knew they had lost hope. Sometimes others of us working for peace continue, but the real belief that we can make a difference has gone. We just go through the motions.

For me anger can give rise to hope. The internal fury that comes from seeing the resources of the earth plundered, or from political leaders using the first person singular 'I' when talking about 'their' government in a supposedly democratic state, or as a bicyclist seeing long lines of cars each with one person in them jamming up roads and polluting the air: all of these give energy for struggle, for building alternatives.

I also gain hope by knowing that our longed for future is a mirage unless we can make some of it happen now, wherever we are. Within ourselves, yes, and also within our small groups, meetings and organisations, we can consciously make our vision a reality: fairness, equality of power, empathy, compassion, conflict creatively used, critical thinking, courage.

Margaret Mead's well quoted phrase remains true: 'Never doubt that a small group of committed citizens can change the world.' I have seen many such groups help to rekindle lost hope in others, just by contact.

Hope, if it is not simply optimism, needs also to be grounded in a sense of the huge variety of alternatives. Think of the top-down nature of our global order, in which power is held by a few, most of whom are predominantly white, older, male, Anglo-Saxon and Christian, at least nominally. Imagine now a bottom-up world, globalisation from the bottom up. Imagine taking democracy seriously. Imagine the reinvention of local authorities, the state, companies, civil society, the media, in which all are freed from the shackles of financial and corporate interests and are focused on human needs and security. Imagine a UN with a people's assembly to complement and perhaps oversee the General Assembly. Imagine . . . the sentiments in John Lennon's song will not die.

We can see aspects of all these developments already happening. The ban on landmines, reductions in international debt, the setting up of the international criminal court, the successful public campaign for drugs companies to make AIDS drugs available more cheaply, the agreement to control the sale of 'conflict diamonds', are all examples of global changes brought about by extensive popular activity and pressure. We have seen the huge potential changes which can result from the mobilisation of people against the invasion of Iraq. We all know cases from our own experience.

Is there anything that can stop these cases from multiplying?

However, we will certainly need also to find ways to protect our hope. Any sane look at the next decade or more, extrapolating from existing trends, will have to include the likelihood of much increased levels of violence and misery. For many of us these will come much closer to home than previously. We may need to prepare ourselves in our meetings and communities: to talk about what might take place and think about our responses to it, so that when the worst happens we maintain our sanity, our faith and our capacity to act.

SIGNPOSTS ❯

The next and penultimate chapter of this book moves on from considering ourselves primarily as individuals and global citizens to looking at our Quaker institutions. They are the public face of Quakerism. If we are called to respond creatively, within and without, what can we expect of our Yearly Meeting and our other institutions? Are there more effective ways in which they can enable us, and the Society as a whole, to witness to peace and justice? Small as we are, can we make our smallness more beautiful?

8

Building peace
through the Society of Friends

If we are beginning to sketch out a future which is more assertive and more courageously nonconformist than for a good while, we need to organise: we cannot be signs of contradiction on our own. In our global society, we have seen that growing militarisation and the doctrine of 'preemptive intervention' are making aggression and war increasingly acceptable in order to advance political aims. Dominant trends in our society in Britain make it unpopular to challenge attitudes and structures which exclude people, or keep them in poverty, here or overseas. For many of us, our own comfortable lifestyles make it hard to accept the cost to our resources and our respectability that such contradiction is likely to entail.

At the same time, on a spiritual level, advances in our understanding of the nature of knowledge and experience mean that we live in a world of relativism, where no objectivity is ultimately possible, no truth, religious or otherwise, goes unchallenged, or can claim *a priori* acceptance. Our witness to that of God within everyone, our commitment to peace, equality and justice have all to be interpreted afresh, justified in today's terms and, crucially, upheld in creative action if the Society is not to wither and become a historical footnote.

I want to think freely therefore about what we need from our Quaker institutions, and do so from the perspective of an activist. I have chosen to start from the need rather than from what we already have. Those with more direct knowledge may want to relate this to the current institutional reality of Britain Yearly Meeting.

At the outset I want to acknowledge the superb work and commitment of so many who serve Britain Yearly Meeting. I know many of them personally. What follows is intended to provide food for thought to enable us to take these achievements further.

What do we need from the Society?

My question, then, is how can the Society help its members, corporately and institutionally, to work for peace and justice? What do we need from it that cannot be provided from other sources?

Often, for me, my response to a question begins as a feeling. As I ponder this question I feel one emotion above all: loneliness. I feel, as a Quaker working outside the Society's institutions, essentially on my own. The main working link I have with Quakerism is through remarkable individuals – many of them members of my local meeting – who, entirely of their own volition, and often from their own pockets, support the work of RTC in practical ways. Without them, both inside and outside the organisation, we would not have been able to sustain it through these past twelve years.

But I lack a sense of being on the journey with 'Quakerdom', with the body of other Quakers who share the same deep inspiration, and have similar values and vision. And this is what I need, most profoundly. Without this sense of companionship I risk losing touch, losing energy, losing contact with the original source of my commitment, with what ultimately, for me, gives my work meaning.

And I dare to imagine there are many of us with similar feelings. As I write these words I have just returned from a visit to Zimbabwe, where Jane and I were able to visit a range of people, including Richard and Pushpa Knottenbelt (see Chapter 1). In the midst of a collapsing, impoverished society they are continuing to uphold Quaker values in their work as teachers and to live lives of integrity, but at huge cost as raging inflation destroys people's values along with their money, and violence, latent or overt, is never far away. While they have many sources of strength, Quaker companionship of the kind I have mentioned could be so helpful for them, but they have no local meeting and the Society as a whole in Zimbabwe is weak.

Accompaniment

So, from the Society writ large, I hope for, in one word, accompaniment. Looking back, I can see how blessed I have been in the past with people, many but certainly not all Quakers, who have accompanied me in a variety of ways. Broadly the companionship of these people has manifested itself in three main ways: support, challenge and inspiration. Very often these have been interventions for which I did not ask, nor, in many cases, did I know what I needed until it was offered. What a delight it was to be supported by an offer of 'mad money' by a local trust: this turned out to be £50 (in the early 1980s) to be used to enhance the life and spirit of the world studies curriculum project I was engaged in, but it could not be spent on any practical needs of the work. Sometimes the accompaniment presented a challenge which was not welcome, but which made me ask searching questions of myself: Quakers in Kinshasa, very new to the Society and desperately poor, would ask me frequently how I could be a Quaker, with its unique fusion of faith and action, and yet so unwilling, in the parlous state of Zaire as it was then, to talk about Quakerism and persuade others to join the Society. Adam Curle's Swarthmore Lecture *True Justice* opened a new world of peacemaking to me, evocative and inspirational with its eclectic mix of academic rigour and spiritual insight, at a time when I was wondering what direction to take.

The journey we have sketched out in this book requires determination, courage, insight and faith. The Society can become again a prophetic community, living out the future today, embodying in its life and that of its members the future it wishes to see, exemplifying values which its founders, both Quaker and Christian, point unerringly to.

But our vision of how we should live today, our practical direction, is not contained in any blueprint, biblical or otherwise. Quakers do not believe in a single revelation, encapsulated for all time in the Word. Rather our experience is of a continually evolving revelation, which we discover by 'living adventurously' and being attentive to the 'promptings of love and truth in our hearts'. Christ himself interpreted this for us for his time. He undoubtedly directed his ministry to the time in which he lived, and to the future he hoped passionately for. For us the basics remain, but how they are to be lived needs to be continually rethought in the light of historical change.

Peace witness and work for social justice, while guided by the same fundamentals as when the Society began, are very different in their practical manifestation now from the time of George Fox or Elizabeth Fry. If we are to live our lives in the same truth and inspiration which they experienced, we need help. But we will need more companionship, active and searching, manifesting at least these dimensions of support, challenge and inspiration.

Fusing worship and struggle

I am looking for companionship with radical people who are willing to bring worship into the heart of social and political struggle. I am looking for a systematic sharing of spiritual insight, which confronts me afresh with the reality of the Love which suffuses and surrounds us and challenges me to set my current life alongside the response to that Love which I could be making.

This need not take a pious or overly serious form. A number of us will remember well radical Christian periodicals of the nineteen-sixties such as the *Catonsville Roadrunner*, which contained cartoons and humorous snippets alongside penetrating articles about the political realities of the day, news of nonviolent direct actions and items designed to make readers question their existing and perhaps conventional social and political responses to the Christian message. It is an interesting commentary on our day that there seems to be nothing similar available to us from contemporary radicals which combines radical political action with a spiritual perpective. The magazine *Resurgence* is perhaps the nearest we have, but it is gentle, rather short on humour, and barely raises the temperature. I am still searching for material of this nature amongst Quaker literature.

If the Society is to provide such an accompaniment for its members and others, it will need to dig deeper wells for its members to drink from. It will place spiritual renewal as close to its heart as social and political witness. It will tend to both needs, yet unite them as one in reality, as Quakers have always witnessed to. It will resist a tide that seems to be running in some places which sees spiritual renewal as quite separate from action, politics and living witness, as though one could become a finer, more spiritual person in splendid isolation from the messy world which surrounds us.

Deepening in the Spirit

Multifarious approaches are needed to help us put worship at the heart of life, wherever we are, despite the 'time-bankrupt' nature of the lives that many of us lead. One manifestation of this could involve creating more spaces in more accessible times and places, where all of us, Quakers and like-minded friends living and acting in the world, can refresh ourselves, reflect again on our work and witness in the world, and be challenged with our own Quaker history and inspiration to risk more, to extend our limits. It could mean making common cause with those of other faiths who are also sensing the need to end our complicity in a system out of control. It could involve making more space for, and finding ways to nourish members who are attending to the roots of our faith and its relation to the world, encouraging them to deepen their search and reach out to the Society at large. It is encouraging that much of this is already happening. It is discouraging that it is so small in relation even to the size of the membership. A prophetic Quaker community is going to require that these opportunities become much more widely available, and make them happen with their own efforts.

Such a depth of worship will affect the way we see the world, and the way we live in it. And it will inevitably provide inspiration: a calling forth of and renewing of vision and hope, a counter to the despair which people working for peace and justice can easily fall prey to.

Deepening the witness

The accompaniment I seek will inevitably foster a wider involvement in peace and social witness, and create a thirst to learn from others, wherever they may be, who are engaged in peace and social action. It is my strongest hope that it will also create a similar thirst to learn honestly from the experience of itself as a body and that of us, its members.

Britain Yearly Meeting has tended, human as it is after all, to be rather unwilling to share those things which do not apparently succeed. When Jane and I took up our Quaker Representative post in Botswana in the early 1980s we were explicitly required, without explanation, not to contact the previous Quaker workers in the area. Of course it made us all the keener to do so.

While I am sure that things have changed greatly from that time, if you look at *Quaker News* today, you could be forgiven for thinking that everything the Society undertakes is a sparkling success, except for its dwindling membership and income. And yet I am sure I am not alone in noticing that in this field, as in most human endeavour, most efforts lead to unexpected outcomes, and often to 'failure'. Indeed, fortunately, it is from our 'failures' that we often learn the most. I doubt if Quaker Peace and Social Witness is seriously different.

Action-research rather than success and failure

With a deeper sense of why we are doing what we do, and a growing self-confidence, I live in hope that the Society will come to lose its fear of failure. Instead it will begin to reframe its work less in terms of success and disaster and view it with more equanimity as 'action-research'. From this vantage point, peacebuilding is no longer a set of more or less separate pieces of work or projects which either succeed or do not. Instead it describes a process, work which we undertake in faith, certainly with the closest possible attention to preparation and strategy, but ultimately recognising that we are not in control of what works and does not.

With this more lateral thinking, process-focused perspective, all our peace work can be seen as practical action-research, whose outcomes – intended or not, failures especially as well as successes – are important for our own work, and for the field of conflict transformation as a whole to advance. With this perspective, honesty and openness become priorities, and advantages, above the understandable wish for confidentiality.

And yet we will still need to be rigorous with ourselves about assessing and reassessing how we are doing. We will always need to question whether we are doing the best we can, and implementing our learning into our work.

If we can move towards this more transparent approach, essential if we are to learn from our experience and share the outcomes with like-minded others, we will need to overcome the potentially serious problem with funders, who as yet have less incentive to see 'failures' as learning experiences. They might however already have been put off by a renewed Society with a less conventional, more assertive peace and social witness agenda. In which case we will need to find new sources of finance amongst those who are willing to take this more radical, but also ultimately more realistic stance.

Can Quaker work be done by non-Quakers?

If the Society moves in this direction, we may come to ask whether paid Quaker peace work – in the sense of work undertaken in and out of Quaker faith – can really be done by non-Quakers, unless at least they have a reasonably deep faith commitment which is similar to that held by Quakers. Certainly the more visible, social role can be performed by anyone with the right skills and aptitudes. But this role is then indistinguishable from peace work undertaken by many agencies with a social agenda. What is it that people outside the Society see in Quakers? How do they see us as different? Answers to these questions may help us to see what we need in our workers of the future, and to leave posts unfilled, or be prepared to hand them on to other agencies, if we do not find such people.

My own view is that Quakers need to find from amongst ourselves people who are fitted to do the work we or our institutions have identified. This work will be both spiritual and social, personal and political, and be rooted in our testimonies for peace and equality.

Influencing and advocacy

As a more vital accompaniment of peace and justice workers (loosely defined) begins to take place amongst members of the Society, assisted by our meetings and institutions at local and national levels, we will be better placed to build on our long tradition of associating with governments, and 'speaking truth to power'. We continue to need Quakers to facilitate, influence and lobby at the political levels. The Society has been performing this function well for a long period, in Northern Ireland, through the Quaker United Nations Offices and Quaker Council for European Affairs, and elsewhere: promoting values of nonviolence, disarmament, tolerance and social justice. This witness will need to be further strengthened and sharpened if the Society is to adopt a more assertive approach towards peace and conflict transformation work in general.

A world without weapons

As we do this Quakers will continue to stand for a world without weapons. We take this position ultimately out of our faith: because it is right rather than because it works. We are prepared to pay the price of this commitment if need be. In the course of this witness a major role of the Society is to point up the 'myth' that violence works (as we have seen earlier).

Not only do we work for a world without weapons. We also work for, and believe in, the possibility of a world without violence of any kind, without domination. A world in which there is no abuse or beating, no rape or battering, no assertion of power through gender, race, age, sexual orientation or physical abilities. A world in which humankind does not abuse the planet, but cares for and enhances the life-giving biosphere.

Another dimension of this witness consists in exposing for the wider public the real horrors of war. Most Naation staaates that engage in wars today try hard to conduct them out of the gaze of the general public, who are fed highly censored stories and images. Despite, or perhaps because of, the presence of 700 journalists 'embedded' in US and British military formations during the most recent Gulf War, much of the misery and devastation was overlooked. The perspective taken was often (with some notable exceptions) one of 'us' and 'them', with a tacit or more overt viewpoint that 'we' are justified and 'they' are either criminals or hapless victims. Casualties on 'our' side were often described (but the true reality not seen), while Iraqi deaths were largely invisible, and numbers unknown. When Al Jazeera, the Arabic television station, carried pictures of Iraqi civilian bodies mutilated by a purported strike from US forces, the cry of 'unfair play' was loud from British and American officialdom. The palpable fear was that if the public really saw the horrors being perpetrated in their name, they would no longer agree to support the war.

It is hard for people to imagine the horror of what actually takes place. How then can they take a view about the desirability of warfare as a means of resolving conflict? Can Quakers make more of a contribution here?

It will be important too to look for ways to build links between the separate lobbies and movements for peace, development, rights and the environment. It is insane and divisive that these fields maintain such separate identities. To the outsider their underlying unity is hard to find, and they are frequently rivals for public funds, yet they are rooted in the same movement for a safer, sustainable world society, and activists move easily from one part of the field to another. Could we envisage a new Coalition for Global Survival, incorporating these different elements and working around the issue common to us all? Is it possible to envisage the Society of Friends taking an initiative to create such a Coalition?

From amateurs to professionals?

Much of this book could be understood as a barely veiled proposal that Quakers should become more professional in their approach to peacebuilding.

To use words such as amateur and professional may or may not be helpful: for some it may conjure up associations which bring back a nostalgia for amateurism, when sport was played for the love of the game, rather than for the money. An amateur would rather lose than break the rules on purpose. Amateurs only train when they have time, and do not mind too much if they achieve their goals or not.

Professionals on the other hand are serious about winning. A 'professional foul' in football occurs when a player breaks the rules deliberately in order to gain advantage.

Leaving stereotypes firmly behind, it is indeed possible to see the contents of this chapter as, in effect, suggesting that we need to combine what is best from both traditions, while moving our centre of gravity towards what is best about professionalism. We very much need to maintain the spirit of amateurism, which motivates us with passionate commitment to the process of peacebuilding and encourages us to enjoy what we do, to value and celebrate the unique contribution of each other to the struggle. Amateurs can laugh and enjoy each other's company unashamedly, however serious the circumstances. And with laughter comes healing.

Professionalism, on the other hand, tells us that we are in for the long haul. We cannot lay down a piece of work because we have lost our enthusiasm, or simply because it does not seem to be working, tempting though that might be. Professionalism teaches us to do our analysis, to manage our work efficiently, to inform ourselves actively about the growing experience and wisdom of others in this field, to seek and sustain alliances with others, to evaluate as we go along, to stop before we are exhausted and burnt out. And it tells us that being effective is important; it is not enough to say that we acted in faith, and left the results to God.

At the same time our professionalism is hollow if we do not place at the centre a deep commitment to honest and respectful relationships. In so doing we must expect difficulties, and what may sometimes seem to be betrayal. In one aid programme I was responsible for, I came to rely heavily on a colleague whom 1 had brought into the organisation and trained and nurtured for some two years. I discovered too late that once my trust was gained he had begun to defraud the organisation. Whole projects were invented, as I belatedly discovered when trying to visit them. For some time afterwards 1 was devastated and unable to trust other colleagues. But it was their example and support which ultimately helped me see the fruits of trust, and come to terms with the inevitable casualties.

This whole debate serves to raise questions about the level of quality and commitment needed if we are to live up to our calling. Quakers have a vocation to be in the vanguard of peace work. Our history demonstrates it, the situation demands it. We need to change gear, to re-orientate ourselves and to see again now where our particular niche lies.

This will necessitate much reflection, and the outcome cannot be prejudged. However, Quaker Peace and Social Witness has been rethinking its approach for some time, and there are some positive signs.

If there is a change in the direction I have been advocating it will necessitate the Society's institutions accepting more of a leadership role than they seem to have been willing to exercise in the recent past. There seems at present to be an acceptance among many that Britain Yearly Meeting structures not only exist to *serve* the members of the Society – undeniably so – but generally to *obey* them, to do their bidding. This way, if taken to its ultimate, can lead to stagnation: paid staff, immersed in their fields with time to explore ideas and interact widely, have access to new thinking and experience not available to most members. We risk becoming rather cautious, just at a time when we need to be more adventurous. I live in hope that our institutions will provide bold leadership, bringing spirit and struggle together in a new form of accompaniment, so that our structures and meetings, both local and national, act above all as *enablers* to all who pick up the challenge to live out our truth.

What does the Society need from us?

If much of this chapter has attempted to answer the question 'What do we need from the institutions of the Society?' it is pertinent to ask also 'What then, do the institutions of the Society need from us?' I would refer the reader to the main body of this book. If we, members of the Society and sympathisers, can renew ourselves, and have the courage to live the social and political implications in our lives, we will have done what is needed to enable Quakers to become again a people who not only speak truth, but embody it boldly as prophetic witness.

9

Are we listening?

Early Christian monks warned their followers against Pernicious Peace. They did not of course mean that we should be fighting each other all the time. The danger they saw was that in our search for peace we would settle for the easy life, for inner peace and quiet, when the peace they knew was full of striving and struggle.

The path they saw was strewn with boulders and potholes. If travellers avoided them they missed the point of the journey.

Today, in a similar manner, we need the obstacles, for our outer as well as inner journeys. They are the places where we are challenged, as our values and beliefs bring us into potential conflict with things that are happening around us. When we oppose a war, propose a more humane way of receiving asylum seekers, or join an initiative to address local community divisions we become signs of contradiction. In joining with others in conspiring, and then confronting a particular issue or injustice we both chart out another stretch of our own journey and offer a signpost to others, to respond to as they wish.

For there certainly is not one pathway which we must all tread. We have seen enough in this small book alone of the range of work that peacebuilding involves, from the inner to the outer, from the activist to the hermit. We all have different talents and aptitudes. Each of us is forging our own path. It crosses and recrosses that of others in many places, but remains our own personal journey.

And here we can free ourselves of the need to 'save the world'. Our task is to start where we are, where the indignation or the anger points to, and follow the Light as we see it, in company with others. We will act, even though the relationship between cause and effect is convoluted and the act in itself will not stop the injustice. Every action has a global resonance, at both spiritual and political levels. To challenge the disadvantage and exclusion of a group in our locality in a strategic, sustained way is to work for peace, as surely as joining a campaign against arms sales. In many ways it is harder to do: the nearer we perceive our frontline to be, the more choices confront us, and the more potentially life transforming are our responses.

George Fox's call still resounds: 'Be patterns, be examples in all countries, places, islands, nations, wherever you come, that your courage and life may preach among all sorts of people...then you will come to walk cheerfully over the world, answering that of God in every one' (Fox, ed. Nickalls p.263; *Quaker faith & practice* 1995 §19.32).

As we struggle, the Spirit will draw us forward, towards the most loving, courageous journey we are capable of. Such a journey may be increasingly full of risk, bringing us into conflict with our own secular society, perhaps costing us our respectability, as individuals and as a Religious Society. Meeting for Sufferings, these days principally the Quaker standing executive body, could yet have to live up to its name again.

As we accept this challenge we will need to overcome our (for the most part) middle class British reluctance to make a fuss, to expose ourselves to ridicule. We know this. We have seen that others are there with us, before us, in other parts of the world as well as our own, with knowledge and expertise we can share, and add to in our turn. We can reach out to them, network together, act in concert with them.

And yet . . . the gradually warming frog still refuses to jump from the saucepan. What is it then that stops us from moving, challenging more energetically this culture of domination and violence in which we live? Why is there apparently so much resistance?

Four factors seem to me to stand out.

Guilt

One factor for some may be guilt. The British history of empire, and all that went with enforcing it, is still with us. For white British people the presence of different ethnic communities is a painful reminder of what was done, and of the way immigration was, and continues to be, handled. In the face of deprivation today, especially amongst black communities, there is a sense of guilt which can lead both to hyperactivity and paralysis. We can usefully become more self-aware about this, talk about it, and differentiate between guilt and responsibility. Guilt is a result of identifying with a history which we could not in fact have influenced. We were not there. It was not our fault. We can, however, accept responsibility for the current situation, and for righting wrongs where we can, within the limitations which we all have.

Complicity

The pervasive world system has an invisible dimension, its own outstations, lodged within our own psyches. When we look at the motor which has brought us together in our global village it is, as we have seen, primarily the market, furnished by global capitalism. At that market we are each of us consumers. Without us the system will fall. We have been educated to behave as loyal servants of a system driven by the urge for power and profit, which seeks dominance by any means necessary. That is bad enough, given the implications for world resources of a never-ending supply of new goods.

Delusion

Just as insidious, however, is the message we have been drip-fed with since childhood: the more you have the happier you are. It is such an apparently innocuous message on a small scale, but the system makes us its captives so easily. How quickly our sense of self-worth comes to depend on what possessions, qualifications and knowledge we have. Our egos require a regular fix of consumption, and a favourable comparison with significant others.

Of course we can be inverted consumers, gaining our sense of worth from thanking God that we are not like others. But that is hardly something to be proud of either, and makes us still prisoners of the system.

Ambivalence

These factors can make us deeply ambivalent about challenging the way the world works. Many of us benefit from it, we are fed daily with its messages through the media, we often unthinkingly behave in accordance with its wishes. It disempowers us as we strive to become agents of change and peace. It allows us to lead our lives as if tomorrow will be the same as yesterday, while the evidence accumulates that tomorrow is a step nearer to the breakdown of life systems on earth.

What can free us of bonds such as these?

How can we be unlocked, and become free to act? We will all have our ideas, and there are no finalities here. For me, imagination, perhaps, and in particular its sister empathy can provide some of the keys: making the leap to be in another's shoes, to feel what that is really like. Empathy – solidarity – with the oppressed other is what we suppress every day when we pass beggars outside our shops, glance at bored teenagers on the street corner, or see, on our screens, women and men, young and old, suffer as casualties of war, or through grinding poverty. Empathy is what governments seek to avoid at all costs when they refuse to accept that terrorism has human reasons behind it.

It is empathy that shows me who really are my brothers and sisters: people like me though not like me, endowed with the same human spirit, homes for the same loves, and the same Love. If I make that leap, and welcome them as myself, where can I stop? What will I not do to help them? What will I not do, still in the spirit of love, to change the hearts of those who threaten them?

Living and acting in the Spirit of Truth and Love, we know we can challenge the powers that be, in ourselves and beyond. Small steps, one at a time. Spirited Living is our calling. Our children and grandchildren, born and unborn, echo the call. Are we listening?

Some questions for reflection

1. The title of this book, *Spirited Living*, reflects a particular view about peace and justice work. It is no longer 'over there', if it ever was. Peace begins here and now, wherever we are. How does this speak to you? What possibilities does it suggest, personally and for your meeting?

2. In Chapter 5 it is suggested that conflict is integral to a well-functioning organisation. How does your meeting deal with conflict? In what ways could the meeting learn practically from the ideas presented here?

3. In Chapter 6, it is suggested that members of the Society need to be more willing to stand out if they are to be faithful to our peace witness: to contradict, confront, conspire in order, ultimately to make the space for fruitful conversations. How are these ideas useful? Can you see ways in which you and others in your meeting might take them up?

4. How far does Chapter 7, Acting out of Concern, reflect your experience? Which aspects of it can you apply to your own life, and that of your meeting?

5. Should the central structures of the Society try to be more enabling, in the sense conveyed in Chapter 8? How would you like them to be?

6. In what ways does your meeting support work for peace and justice? In the light of this lecture, how, if at all, should it change its current focus and level of effort?

Recommended reading
including publications referred to in this book

ACTION, *Transforming Conflict: Reflections of Practitioners Worldwide*, ACTION for Conflict Transformation, 2003.
Written by practitioners belonging to the global ACTION network, it contains insights and experience from myriad initiatives to address social and political conflict. Available from RTC.

Alinsky, Saul, *Rules for Radicals*, Vintage, 1989.
Impassioned advice, from a North American perspective, on how to effect constructive social change. See also Reveille for Radicals, same author and publisher.

Augustine, Saint, Bishop of Hippo, *Confessions*, translated with an introduction by R. S. Pine-Coffin, Penguin, 1961.

Bailey, Sydney, *Peace is a Process*, London: Quaker Home Service, 1993 (Swarthmore Lecture).

Biko, Steve, *I Write What I Like: Selected Writings*, ed. Aelred Stubbs, University of Chicago Press, 1996.

Crafts, Nick, *Britain's Relative Economic Performance, 1870–1999*, Institute of Economic Affairs, 2002.

Curle, Adam, *True Justice: Quaker Peace Makers and Peace Making*, Quaker Home Service, 1981 (Swarthmore Lecture).

Curle, Adam, *To Tame the Hydra: Undermining the Culture of Violence*, Oxford: Jon Carpenter, 1999.
A close look at the world system, its impact on us psychologically as well as economically and politically, and options for challenging it, from a Buddhist/Quaker viewpoint.

de Waal, Frans, *Peacemaking among Primates*, Harvard, 1989.

Fox, George, *The Journal of George Fox*, ed. John L. Nickalls, 1952; current edition London: Quaker Home Service, and Philadephia: Philadelphia Yearly Meeting, 1997.

Freeman, Laurence, *Jesus the Teacher Within*, Continuum, 2000.
A searching book addressing questions about meaning and identity in the light of Jesus' life and teaching. One chapter describes the tradition and method of meditation as promoted by the Christian Meditation Centre.

Galtung, Johan, *The True Worlds, A Transnational Perspective*, New York: Free PR, 1980.
Profound analysis of how world disorder can give way to inter-dependence and peace.

Galtung, Johan: 'Cultural Violence', in *Journal of Peace Research* vol.27 no.3 (1990), pp.291–305.

Hanh, Thich Nhat, *The Miracle of Mindfulness*, Beacon Press, 1987.
Practical and inspiring, offering skills and methods to become more aware, more mindful in everyday life.

Heaney, Seamus, *The Cure at Troy* (1990) in *Opened Ground: Poems 1966–1996*, Faber, 1998.

Konner, Melvin, *The Tangled Wing, Biological Constraints on the Human Spirit*, Times Books, 2002.
A profound look at human nature, and the potential for positive change, from a wide-ranging scientific point of view.

Layard, Richard, 'What would make a happier society?' in *The Lionel Robbins Memorial Lectures* 2002/3 (Lecture 3, 5 March 2003, p. 19). http://cep.lse.ac.uk/events/lectures/layard/RL050303.pdf

Lerner, Michael, 'The Ten Commitments', on website: www.tikkun.org/renewal/index.cfm/action/ten_commitments.html San Francisco: Tikkun Community.

Miall, Hugh, Oliver Ramsbotham and Tom Woodhouse, *Contemporary Conflict Resolution*, Polity Press, 1999.
A very readable overview of the field of conflict transformation and peacebuilding, dealing lucidly with theory, always with an eye to reality and the implications for action.

Monbiot, George, *The Age of Consent: A Manifesto for a New World Order*, Flamingo 2003.
Ingenious practical solutions to the world's problems, from a utopian realist.

Quaker faith & practice: the book of Christian discipline of the Yearly Meeting of the Religious Society of Friends (Quakers) in Britain, Britain YM, 1995; 2nd ed, 1999.

Responding to Conflict and Coalition for Peace in Africa, *The Wajir Story*, Birmingham: Responding to Conflict, 1999.

Responding to Conflict (Simon Fisher, Dekha Ibrahim Abdi, Jawed Ludin, Richard Smith, Steve Williams, Sue Williams), *Working with Conflict, Skills and Strategies for Action*, Responding to Conflict (RTC) and Zed Books, 2000.
A source book of practical tools, ideas and techniques for tackling conflict arising out of RTC's work worldwide. Available from RTC in several languages.

Joseph Rowntree Foundation: Report, 2003.

Theatre Workshop, Charles Chilton and members of the original cast, *Oh! What a Lovely War*, Methuen Drama, 1993.
A theatrical chronicle of the First World War, told through the songs and documents of the period. First performed by Joan Littlewood's Theatre Workshop at the Theatre Royal, Stratford East, London in 1963.

Twist, Lynne, 'Waging peace: a story about Robert Muller', in *West by Northwest* online magazine, posted 14 March 2003 www.westbynorthwest.org/artman/publish/article_340.shtml

Wink, Walter, *The Powers That Be, Theology for a new Millennium*, Doubleday, 1998.
A passionate book which urges us to rethink our world view, and the scope for nonviolent action, from a radical, justice-oriented Christian perspective.